WHEN ROTTEN THINGS HAPPEN

Helping Adolescents Learn How to Handle Emotionally-Charged Situations

by Rob Kerr

youth light inc.

© 2013 by YouthLight, Inc. | Chapin, SC 29036

Layout and Design by Melody Taylor
Project Editing by Susan Bowman

Library of Congress Control Number
2012952322

ISBN 9781598501278
10 9 8 7 6 5 4 3 2 1
Printed in the United States

To my fine, fine
brothers
Kevin and Jim.

//

About the Author

Robb Kerr as been a long-time teacher and special education consultant with the
Peel Board of Education in Ontario, Canada. *When Rotten Things Happen* is Rob's fifth
published program that incorporates his rational self-instruction approach in emotional
education, along with several journal articles relating to wellness and social-skills
programs. Over the past three decades Rob has conducted numerous educational
workshops throughout Canada and the United States.

Rob presently lives in Guelph, Ontario, Canada, with his wife, Heather,
and black cat, Elmo.

//

Contents

The Lessons //

Introduction

Stress is a very personal thing – much like life itself.

This is no less true for our young people. Stress, for each boy, each girl, is an intimate, deeply personal affair, and dealt with in equally personal ways. Young people need no help in understanding the first two things about stress: one, it feels rotten and two, "I would like it to go away." Or, bottom line, "I would like less of it."

It will help young people to understand that there are really only two sources, two camps, of stress. On the one hand there are those external stressors that relate most directly to those rotten things that are piled on to our plates without our permission – much like homework might be piled on by an insensitive boss or teacher; it's one thing after another and the stress builds as the pile heightens. On the other hand, there is the internal stress that I pile onto myself; it's much like Natalie Goldberg says: "Stress is an ignorant state – it believes that everything is an emergency."

There is little doubt that managing stress, managing rottenness, is a skill. It is learning-thing; it requires a plan. In the absence of a plan, there is panic. As Christian Nevell Bovee describes, "Panic is a sudden desertion of us, and a going over to the enemy of our imagination." Panic is the opposite of calm and strong – and it is a frightening thing for any boy or girl. In some ways it is almost an out-of-body experience: I am acting, but I am not really in control. It is the enemy, panic, who is in control. Not me. Psychologists describe this sudden loss of control as downshifting – when neurons of the limbic system flood the neo-cortex. It is when the emotional brain hijacks the thinking brain. It is when we lose it.

It is not always easy to deal with stressful situations coolly and calmly. And this is especially true for our young people. These are the kids of the information age – arguably more socially aware and technically savvy than any generation before. Yet, in this global village of fast knowledge, instant accesses, and ongoing social networking, learning to manage stress comes back to three basics: stress management (1) involves the learning of practical emotional skills; (2) it requires a community where the young person feels safe and valued; (3) it thrives in the presence of a caring, helping, competent adult.

In our helping roles (as teachers, counselors, social workers, parents) with young people we are often supporting them with their life stresses, with the rottenness that has invaded their lives. *When Rotten Things Happen* is a dynamic program of emotional wellness for helping-adults to use with all (or perhaps a targeted group of) students in their pre-and-early adolescent years.

This is a program that is built squarely on a single conviction – the belief that all young people can learn to manage rotten things! More precisely, it is the conviction that they can learn to manage the stress that surely and inevitably comes into their lives. Young people have an inherent resilience; they have great capacity to examine and change their own destructive attitudes, and consequently their behavior, and consequently their emotions.

When Rotten Things Happen endorses and embeds a set of best practices supported by educational research, as well as efficacy studies regarding cognitive-behavioral interventions. The 40 lessons of this unique program strategically and intentionally:

1. **Develop Self Awareness** – by exploring the attitudes and self-talk that are linked to those rotten things that happen to us (to some extent) all the time.

2. **Introduce a Wellness Language** – by identifying and using key terms that lead to an understanding of psychological wellness and behavior change.

3. **Promote Critical Thinking** – by examining those belief systems (that follow rotten events) and actively challenging unproven, irrational and incapacitating self-talk that leads, inevitably, to a timid, unsuccessful under-reaction or to an angry, unsuccessful over-reaction.

4. **Empower All Students** – by teaching the important behavioral-emotional tools that allow students to change their life-habits in a positive direction; by teaching and over-using the Sensible Acting & Thinking (SAT) Plan – a simple, 4-step plan that leads to rational, successful responses to those rotten things that happen; and, by regularly reinforcing attempts by students to use the SAT Plan.

5. **Build Character** – by openly encouraging young people to demonstrate courage, fairness, tolerance, forgiveness and patience – even when others are behaving rottenly to them.

6. **Create a Culture of Respect and Mutual Support** – by implementing (and insisting on) a set of individual and group rights that ensure safety and risk taking and endlessly encourage students to help themselves and each other.

These are the hallmarks of the program. In an atmosphere of safety, encouragement and rational thinking, every child can learn to better manage their own thoughts, emotions and behavior – especially, when rotten things happen.

Rob Kerr

The Ideas

//

When Rotten Things Happen is a program of emotional wellness and enablement. It is all about enabling young people to face up to rotten things - those terrible, no-good, bad-luck, rotten things that happen all the time. And to act wisely.

Yes, Rotten Things Happen!

Sad but true. Rotten things happen to all of us, big and little, brown and pink, strong and weak. Some of these things might seem to be "a little bit rotten" – like missing the bus or over-cooking the pizza or losing a soccer game. There are other things that we may think of as "fairly rotten" – like failing a math test or not being invited to a party or being openly embarrassed in a restaurant. And, there will be other things that will take hold of our emotions in a big way, shake us mightily, those things we may name as "very rotten" – like having a parent die or becoming very sick or losing a close friend. For those of us who are in helping roles with young people it is the first thing to acknowledge and to accept: all rotten things are not created equal.

Nor are rotten things doled out in equally. For sure, bad things happen to all of us, and on the first page of it all, we have to accept that. But, we have to recognize – and accept – the fact that rotten things cling to some of us more than they cling to others. It is part of the less-than-fair reality of the world and it is obvious to young people themselves: bad luck and all forms of things rotten are not doled out in equal shares.

It is also glaringly evident that we do not experience rottenness in quite the same way. One young girl may consider losing a chess tournament to be "greatly rotten," while another may consider that same event to be only "mildly rotten." One boy may experience flying in an airplane as extremely frightening, "a totally rotten thing," whereas another boy will experience that event as extremely thrilling, "a totally wonderful thing." Just as beauty is in the eye of every young beholder, so too is rottenness.

In the middle of difficulty lies opportunity.
- Albert Einstein

Rotten Things Produce Stress

By all indications, stress is on the rise. Professor Lawrence Steinberg (2008) summarizes the research related to what adolescents and parents normally fight about and it may not be about big issues at all. Regardless of the ethnic backgrounds of boys and girls, squabbles in the home relate most often to everyday things like curfews, leisure time activities, clothing, room cleanliness, homework, household chores and choice of friends. Professor Judy Smetana (2011) suggests that a main contributor to all the bickering is the fact that teenagers and their parents define the issues of contention quite differently. Parents are more likely to see the argument issues as matters of what is, by convention, right or wrong; kids, on the other hand, are more likely to see these issues as matters of personal choice.

Nearly all young people consider the time they spend with their friends and classmates to be among the most enjoyable (Csikszentmihalyi & Larsen, 1984). There is no doubt that most young people have a supreme desire to fit in to a social group – and failing to do so is often a real source of stress. Various studies support the fact that popular kids are likely to be socially skilled, intelligent, humorous, and friendly; alternatively, unpopular kids are more likely to be aggressive or withdrawn. Further, boys and girls who are rejected are substantially at risk of developing serious behavioral problems, becoming depressed and dropping out of school. As Lawrence Steinberg makes clear, "Victimization and harassment by peers, whether through physical bullying or relational aggression, have harmful and enduring consequences for individuals mental health."

> There is no doubt that most young people have a supreme desire to fit in to a social group – and failing to do so is often a real source of stress.

It should not be a surprise to any parent or teacher or counselor that all of this stress is affecting the overall wellness of our kids. A 2003 CASA report establishes that kids with high stress levels are twice as likely to smoke, get drunk, and use illegal drugs. More alarming, as the larger body of research is showing, are the links of stress to depression, deviance and suicide. Research at the Oregon National Primate Center presents a strong link between early-life stresses and the incidence of mental health problems during adolescence – and, thus, highlighting the need for proactive interventions with these kids.

A young person will surely find ways of dealing with those daily stressors, those rotten things that happen all the time. Kids learn to cope, one way or another. They may find productive, successful ways of dealing with those rotten things, spending more time with friends, perhaps, or listening to music, or meditating, or spending time alone, or painting a picture, or writing a poem, or playing sports. Yet some of these kids will deal with stress in very negative ways. In her research on teens in distress, Joyce Walker (2005) reports that stressed-out young people who turn to negative life events confess to frequent outbursts of anger, avoidance, or anti-social behaviors. According to Walker, these are the kids who are more likely to break the rules, yell and complain, get drunk, smoke, use doctor-prescribed drugs more frequently, sleep too much, ride around in cars, and cry.

It is not important, nor is it helpful, to make judgments about those rotten things that young people face. It does not matter if an event is, by some adult-thinking standard, truly rotten or not, but it matters greatly that some young person perceives it as rotten. If a teenage girl feels that the acne on her face is "terrible, horrible," then it is that. As a caring, helping adult, I accept that, I start there. If a boy interprets a callous remark about his new clothes as "unbelievably rotten," then it is that. That is where I begin.

The more important point is this: to young people, events are deeply personal. Every unfortunate thing that happens to a boy or girl involves some kind of personal logic about what has happened. Kids make sense of rotten things in different ways. If their own personal logic is largely negative, the young person will in all certainty experience stress. The amount of stress that a boy or girl experiences will most often relate to the nature and degree of negative thinking attributed to the event. If she convinces herself that her acne makes her look "entirely hideous," the girl will undoubtedly experience a great deal of stress.

A Program of Wellness and Enablement

When Rotten Things Happen is first of all a program of psychological wellness and enablement. It is built squarely on the conviction that every child can learn to manage stress more effectively, that kids can learn to help themselves. In caring, supportive, encouraging environments, young people will choose positive life events as a way to cope with the pressures they face, rather than negative life events. The exercises are designed, strategically, to help young people manage the stresses related to those unfortunate, rotten things that happen to them.

In 1920 E. L. Thorndike wrote that social intelligence was all about "acting wisely" in human relations. And that stands nicely as an overall goal of these lessons and experiences – to help kids act wisely in the face of rotten events.

Broadly, there are three over-arching help principles in this book. The first principle was set out in Positively, Learning to Manage Negative Emotions (1987, 1995) and is based on the tenets of my rational self instruction: having young people identify feelings and damaging self-talk related to unfortunate events, examining their unsuccessful responses to the event, and then actively choosing self-talk and action plans that are more rational, more positive, and are likely to be more successful.

The second help principle links to character development – holistically, the importance of acting with strength and integrity. Embedded in each lesson, each simulation, is the message that building strength of character is vital to our wellness – in terms of our self-esteem and in our ability to deal with rotten happenings. The simulations regularly remind the young person to profess courage – and to act courageously; to consider the thoughts and feelings of other people – and to act with fairness; to recognize the inherent dangers in impulsiveness – and to act with patience.

The third help principle of this book relates to the growing body of evidence in psychology that links our general happiness to our social connectedness. It is the idea that young human beings have a need, socially and psychologically, to belong, to be involved in friendships and caring relationships with other people. Each of the exercises in the program actively promotes social connectedness: talking to a parent, a teacher, a counselor, a friend. It is the understanding that caring relationships are central to a young person's wellness.

A Program of Self-Awareness

"A person's sense of self greatly affects how that person functions in the world" (Education for All, 2005).

The psychological wellness of our young people is not so much a destiny or end-product as it is a process. It is a road to travel, an ongoing project of discovery. And, if there is a first step on the road to wellness, to becoming emotionally wise, it points in the direction of self-awareness.

The process of acquiring self-awareness is what Dr. Mel Levine (2002) calls demystification: the idea that young people cannot work on their problems if they do not really understand them – or themselves. And, young people are helped to develop a truer sense of their own selves when they are given a frame of reference, and a working language, to connect themselves and their own strengths, gaps and idiosyncrasies to the outside world.

> The psychological wellness of our young people is not so much a destiny or end-product as it is a process. It is a road to travel, an ongoing project of discovery.

The lessons, here, contribute to a growing awareness of one's self. It is a program that uses simulations and stories to pose important questions: What is stress? Why do some people have a great deal of stress about one specific rotten event, while others have very little stress about that same event? How do my own belief systems and self-talk contribute to my own stress? How do my own action plans affect my stress levels? Is it possible to manage stressful events more effectively? This is a program that encourages young people to reflect on these things, and to have conversations and debates about them. To that end, it is a program that seeks to, little by little by little, demystify the self, and to pave the road for acting wisely in human relations.

A Program of Life Skills

Students need to understand at the outset that acting wisely is directly connected to a set of life skills. Mayer and Salvoey (1993) write that emotional intelligence "is a type of social intelligence that involves the ability to monitor one's own and others' emotions, to discriminate among them, and to use the information to guide one's thinking and actions."

One way or another, all of us have learned – or failed to learn – how to manage and discriminate among emotions. And all of us, one way or another, have learned certain reactions to rotten, stressful happenings. No adult would argue that our young people live day to day in a tumultuous social environment, and it is an unfortunate reality, as Dr. Mel Levine (2001) makes clear, that many of our young people will struggle mightily in their various relationships simply "because they lack social cognition." In essence, the reactions of young individuals to stressful events are a set of learned skills: cognitive skills (how a person has learned to think about the rotten event) and behavioral skills (what a person has learned to do about the rotten event).

While this program recognizes that wise reactions to stress are (in part) skill based, the lessons do not teach those skills in a heavily top-down, or overly didactic manner. Nor is this a program of checklists, rewards and punishments. In these lessons, students are introduced to new concepts and new language, and they are encouraged to use these to create successful responses to the stories and simulations. They will learn new skills – strategies to help them wisely manage the stress of those rotten things that happen – and, as such, they will benefit from feedback, conversation, reflection, experimentation, and opportunities to practice.

The Early Adolescent Brain

Early adolescence is a time of tremendous change, socially, psychologically and physically. At the very outset, it is helpful to understand the biological changes in the adolescent brain.

At about 12 or 13 years old, there are pronounced physical changes taking place in the brain. During this time, there is considerable remodeling of the brain through the processes of synaptic pruning (the gradual elimination of unused connections between the neurons) and myelination (the gradual increase in the protective sheath that encases neural projections). This remodeling takes place, most significantly, in the prefrontal cortex – the area of the young person's brain that is responsible for higher-level thinking, such as planning, decision making, goal setting and metacognition.

Early adolescence, then, is a time of noticeable improvement in abstract thinking. But at the same time, the young person is experiencing changes in her/his limbic system – that area of the brain that plays a key role in emotions. During this time there are steady increases in the levels of neurotransmitters (chemicals such as dopamine and serotonin), which stimulate young individuals to seek higher levels of novelty and excitement, and (in some cases) take more risks.

As Lawrence Steinberg writes in his book, *Adolescence* (2008), "The combination of heightened sensation seeking and a still-maturing prefrontal cortex may make adolescence a period of experimentation with risky activity."

Understanding the adolescent brain helps us to comprehend – and to truly accept – the adolescent herself, himself. On the one hand, there is a certain biological tendency to (at least sometimes) exaggerate the rottenness in events or to over-react to those events. Yet, on the other hand, there is the inherent capacity for young people to reflect more deeply, more profoundly, about how they might respond to unfortunate things in their lives. In the face of all the rottenness out there, each young person has this emerging capability to think more rationally about what is happening, to entertain other ways of making sense of these things, to consider alternate strategies, and (in some cases) to change bad habits.

The Emotional Brain – the Thinking Brain

Why does one young person fly off the handle to a particular rotten event, while another will respond to that same event much more calmly and evenly?

It is often helpful for young people to understand the biology of their own emotional reactions.

In *Emotional Intelligence* (1995) Daniel Goleman refers to the limbic system as our emotional brain and it is a part of our brain that evolved very early. In terms of our survival, this makes sense: urgent, fight-or-flight responses would have allowed us to escape danger or attack prey as necessary.

Young people should understand that lower-order animals, such as fish and reptiles, have no neo-cortex at all. These animals have well-developed emotional brains that allow them lightning responses to smells, sounds, sights or vibrations, but to react without thinking. These animals are not capable of love, affections, or child rearing.

As a human being, with a large prefrontal cortex, each of us has the capability of analyzing stimuli before reacting. We are able to think smartly about our actions; we are able to consider our options – before we react. Still, this does not always happen. There are times when my emotional brain takes over my thinking brain. I react before I think. Goleman describes these as neural highjackings – situations when the emotional brain takes over or floods the thinking brain.

Some of the literature describes this flooding as process of downshifting. In this sense, when a young person feels out of control, or threatened, "the neocortex of the brain tends to shut down (downshift) under threat, and survival mechanisms are activated" (Hart & Leslie, 1983). As Renate Nummela Caine (1997) describes, "When we feel threatened, we downshift our thinking. Downshifted people feel helpless; they don't look at possibilities; they don't feel safe to take risks or challenge old ideas. They have limited choices for behavior." As counselors, educators – and parents – we are called to help young learners break the cycle of flooding, downshifting, by creating safe communities, teaching to the whole

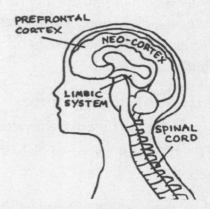

My Emotional Brain

At the very top of my spinal cord is my brain stem – the part of the brain that regulates many of my non-thinking functions, like my breathing and my body metabolism. There is a nerve system that forms a ring around the brain stem; this is called the limbic system and it is the place in my brain that regulates all of my emotions such as love, hate, jealousy, anger, fear, desire, surprise, sadness...all of the feelings that I might have. If I see a spider, the limbic system has the job of alerting my body by sending out neurotransmitters (a bit like electrical impulses) to release body hormones (chemicals). In fact, I have many different kinds of hormones in my body – some to calm me down, some to give me the necessary energy to run or to fight.

child, and regularly promoting higher-order thinking. Caine sums it up precisely: "We understand that children need to be in a community. They need to follow their own interests, and we need to constantly question and challenge them."

The importance of helping young people develop higher-order thinking skills is further supported by the constructionist theories of psychologist, Lev Vygotsky. What happens when something rotten happens to us? According to Vygotsky, our choices for responding to this rotten happening "are limited" when we respond at an "elementary" – or emotional level. But, when a young person gains more self-awareness – particularly in the area of her emotions – she is then able to learn different ways of thinking about that rotten thing. When a young person is helped to generate new plans for dealing with unfortunate events, she becomes a more competent problem solver.

As Vygotsky states, "Higher mental functions allow us to move from impulsive behavior to instrumental action." This is entirely good news for young people who want to manage their own emotions more effectively and it is good news for teachers and counselors who want to help them with that project. A young person can learn to stop an emotional over-reaction; he can learn to think smartly about what has happened and to respond more successfully. When this happens, the thinking brain trumps the emotional brain.

Under-reactions and Over-reactions – Flip Sides of the Same Coin

It is completely obvious that our emotions run on a continuum – low emotional output to high emotional output – and

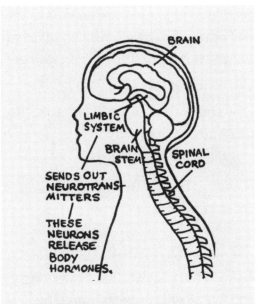

My Thinking Brain
As humans evolved, so did our brain systems. While the brain stem and entire limbic system developed first, the top layers making up the neo-cortex developed last. The prefrontal cortex is that part of my brain which regulates higher-order thinking. As a human being, I have a larger prefrontal cortex than any other animals, and this part of my brain allows me to analyze situations, create options and make complicated decisions.

it might be said that no two individuals will have exactly the same emotional reaction to the same event. Nor will any two individuals act precisely the same way; my feelings, words and actions will always be a little different than anyone else's.

While emotions and actions are unique and nuanced, it greatly helps young people to view these reactions through an easy-to-understand conceptual model. This model is used in many of the lessons and simulations in this program – and it suggests that there are basically three ways to react to a rotten thing: by over-reacting to it; by under-reacting, or by reacting appropriately.

Over-reactions
An over-reaction is when (1) I become too upset and/or (2) when I behave unfairly to others (Kerr, 1995). Such a definition is not intended to be a moral absolute, not at all. Rather, it is a framework for conversation, debate and encouragement.

Young people should understand that an over-reaction is basically a fight response to something rotten that happens to me. If I feel afraid or extremely angry, I may choose to strong arm the problem. I may want to get back at someone, or lash out at something to make it stop. These reactions may be physical (like hurting someone or throwing things) or verbal (like yelling or swearing or threatening).

In the end, an over-reaction is an unwise emotional response that jumps too hard on the problem. It is a response that is too loud, too hurtful, too much. I can rant and rage but at the end of the day the problem is still there!

Under-reactions

If I feel afraid or shy or embarrassed, I may choose to hide from the problem. An under-reaction is not doing enough to deal with the problem. I may want to ignore it, or hide it, or hope that it will go away, or pretend that the problem is not there. It is a bit like the ostrich hiding its head in the sand, thinking that "if I don't see it, the problem is not there."

In the end, an under-reaction is an unwise emotional response that backs away from the problem. It is a response that is too timid, too weak, too little. I can hide my head in the sand but at the end of the day, the problem is still there.

Young people need to understand that over-reactions and under-reactions are NOT opposites – but are flip sides of the same coin.

Both of these reactions should be seen as impulsive, emotionally-charged responses to rotten happenings – and both serve the purpose of reducing stress quickly. And that is the problem – over-reactions and under-reactions are all about a quick fix to managing stress.

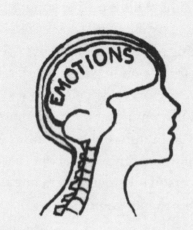

Flooding

There are times when an event can trigger a sudden and strong surge of neurons from the limbic system. If this surge is sudden and strong enough, it may completely flood my neocortex. When my brain is flooded with emotion, I will act before thinking.

The tendency to over-react or under-react to stressful events is almost always counterproductive to a young person's emotional wellness. As life-style choices these reactions need to be seen as desperate, short-term, unsuccessful habits.

Appropriate Reactions

The various exercises and simulations in When Rotten Things Happen repeatedly demonstrate the three important self-reminders of an appropriate reaction; "be calm, be strong, be positive."

There is a deliberate compactness and simplicity to these self-reminders, and it is educationally helpful that the lessons over-use them. Ideally, a young person will internalize these prompts and then generalize them to stressful situations in their own lives. They may ask, "What does it mean to be positive?" Once again, while being positive is an important marker of an appropriate reaction, that term may need qualification and discussion – and, depending on the situation, it may nicely translate into other positive reminders: be safe, be patient, be brave, be fair, be helpful, be respectful, be certain (and it is likely that students themselves will name some others).

When the Emotional Brain Takes Over

What triggers an emotional over-reaction? What causes a person to under-react? Yes, rotten happenings are part of life, and sooner or later they happen to all of us. Yet over-reactions and under-reactions are not part of life. Young people can learn to better manage their emotions when they are helped to see how negative emotions are linked to their own negative thinking.

Negative Self-Talk

In *Humanistic Psychotherapy* (1973), Dr. Albert Ellis points out that human emotions and behaviors are enormously influenced by cognitions, and he makes the blunt statement that "virtually all human disturbance is the result of magical thinking."

It is the position of Dr. Ellis – and the basis of all cognitive therapies – that excessive worry, anger, frustration, and distress are deeply rooted in our own belief systems. In this view, the amount of emotional distress I experience has less to do with the rotten event itself, and more to do with my belief about that rotten event. It is my attitude. What I think. What I tell myself.

It is eminently helpful for any young person to learn that unpleasant emotions are largely the product of negative thinking. My own negative belief system, my own negative self-talk, is likely to trigger my emotional brain, leading to (quite likely) an over-reaction or an under-reaction.

Silly Beliefs, Silly Self-Talk

There are various ways to describe the negative thinking that leads to under-and-over reactions. In his Rational-Emotive Therapy Albert Ellis regularly uses the term irrational belief system or magical thinking to characterize the wrong attitudes that tend to promote emotional distress and bad decision making. My own programs have opted for the more kid-friendly terms, silly beliefs or silly self-talk. In their own way young people easily understand that silly thinking or silly self-talk is illogical, irrational, dangerous, self-defeating, and unsuccessful.

As young people work through the simulations in this program, they should be able to identify the following four qualities or characteristics related to silly beliefs.

Characteristic	Examples
Exaggerated Thinking The tendency to exaggerate the rottenness of an event almost always leads to heightened stress. We sometimes refer to such thinking as awfulizing, terriblizing, or horriblizing. If I tell myself that something is awful, terrible, horrible, then it becomes that.	• Failing that math test would be absolutely terrible! • Her remark to me was awful, awful, awful! • I have to be home at midnight. What a horrible, horrible rule! • If I lose my bike, my parents will kill me! • Saying a speech in front of my whole class is totally rotten. It's the end of the world!
Rigid Thinking The tendency to create rigid or absolute demands invariably leads to attitudes of perfectionism and pervasive guilt. When I tell myself that things absolutely must or should be a certain way, I put myself into a box of stress.	• People should be nice to me all the time – and I can't stand it when they are not! • School should be easy – and I can't stand it when it is not! • I need to get an A in every subject; if I don't, I can't live with myself. • I must be gorgeous all the time; I hate myself when I am not. • I need to wear the best clothes. • I need everybody to like me all the time. • I will only be happy if I am the best player on the team.
Negative Thinking The tendency to think negatively or pessimistically about events invites feelings of sadness and inertia. By deliberately focusing on what is wrong I am manufacturing fear and despondency – and, as a life habit, this should be seen as unhealthy, stifling, and unnecessary.	• It rained on Saturday – and ruined my whole day! • If I try out for that team, I will probably not make it; I am not even going to try. • I have too many freckles; I hate that. • My party will probably be a flop. • That guy is okay, but he bites his nails; I can't stand that. • I am so stupid! • I hate my hair. I am ugly!
Magical Thinking The tendency to think magically relates to a lack of proof- or forming conclusions that are not based on facts or evidence or truth. Most often, magical thinking relates to irrational fears and leads to unnecessary stress.	• If I don't dress nicely, no one will like me. • Look at my hair! Everyone will think I am totally ugly. • If I try and fail, I am a loser! • They were talking about me at lunch today. They all hate me. • If I fail that test, I will be destroyed. • My parents will never get over this! • I can't stand this! • Failing a test proves that I am stupid.

The various simulations that are presented in When Rotten Things Happen regularly and deliberately expose the silly, irrational self-talk of the fictionalized characters. It is educationally vital that students are given the opportunity to discuss and debate these things. Yes, debate and discussion should be an ongoing part of these lessons! Students benefit immensely when they learn and apply new language, new concepts, to their problem solving. And, by sharing the above categories of silly thinking with students, they are better equipped to agree, disagree, analyze, share examples, and expand on these concepts.

Promoting Sensible Thinking

My Rational Self-Instruction (RSI) approach was formulated in Positively! *Learning to Manage Negative Emotions* (Kerr, 1987) and further developed in subsequent programs. As a program of psychological wellness, RSI helps students to recognize their own debilitating silly thinking, to understand the harmful relationship of negative self-talk and over-reactions – and, finally, to actively substitute rational thinking and planning as strategies to solving problems. The rational-emotive approach is summed up by Dr. Ellis: "It encourages them to feel strong appropriate emotions – such as sorrow, regret, unpleasant social conditions" rather than "certain self-defeating and inappropriate emotions – such as guilt, depression, rage, or feelings of worthlessness."

The widely-used approach to helping young people to change their own undermining attitudes is known as cognitive restructuring. In his program, *Exploring Feelings*, (2004) Dr. Tony Atwood explains: "Cognitive restructuring enables the child or adult to correct distorted conceptualizations and dysfunctional beliefs." In a similar way, the various simulations in *When Rotten Things Happen* prompt young people to recognize – and actively substitute – belief systems that are more positive and rational.

The table on the next page takes the previous examples of silly self-talk and morphs each of them into sensible self-talk – beliefs that are more positive, more rational, more successful.

RSI helps students to recognize their own debilitating silly thinking, to understand the harmful relationship of negative self-talk and over-reactions.

Silly Beliefs	Sensible Beliefs
• Failing that math test would be absolutely terrible!	• Failing that math test would be disappointing, but I would get over it.
• Her remark to me was awful, awful, awful!	• That remark was rude, that's all.
• I have to be home at midnight. What a horrible, horrible rule!	• Home at midnight – a drag, but not the end of the world.
• If I lose my bike, my parents will kill me!	• My parents will be upset – but we will all get over it.
• Saying a speech in front of my whole class is totally rotten. It's the end of the world!	• Saying a speech makes me nervous – but there are much worse things.
• People should be nice to me all the time – and I can't stand it when they are not!	• Some people are nice, some are not – that's just he way it is. It is disappointing when people are not.
• School should be easy – and I can't stand it when it is not!	• School is the way it is – I can learn to live with that.
• I need to get an A in every subject; if I don't, I can't live with myself.	• I don't have to be perfect to be good. I will always respect myself.
• I must be gorgeous all the time; I hate myself when I am not.	• My job in life is not to be gorgeous all the time or to impress everyone.
• I need to wear the best clothes.	• I might want nice clothes – but I do not need them.
• I need everybody to like me all the time.	• I can learn to like myself even when others do not.
• I will only be happy if I am the best player on the team.	• I can't always be the absolute best in anything – but that's okay.
• It rained on Saturday – and ruined my whole day!	• The rain can only ruin my day if I let it. I can find other things to do.
• If I try out for that team, I will probably not make it; I am not even going to try.	• I might make the team, I might not. If I don't, I will respect myself having the courage to try.
• I have too many freckles; I hate that.	• Freckles – no need to make that a big deal.
• My party will probably be a flop.	• My party is going to be a smash!
• That guy is okay, but he bites his nails; I can't stand that.	• There are a lot of things I like about that guy. I am not going to let his nail biting be such a big deal.
• I am so stupid!	• I am smart at many things.
• I hate my hair. I am ugly!	• Maybe I can do something else with my hair. I am cute.

• If I don't dress nicely, no one will like me.	• In truth, people like people who are honest and caring. Even so, I don't need people to approve of me all the time.
• Look at my hair! Everyone will think I am totally ugly.	• That's an exaggeration. Not everyone will think I am ugly. They may tease me, but I can deal with that.
• If I try out for that team and fail, I am a loser!	• The truth is: I might make the team. If not, I am a winner for having the courage to try.
• They were talking about me at lunch today. They all hate me.	• There is no proof that they were talking about me. There is no proof that they all hate me.
• If I fail that test, I will be destroyed.	• If I fail that test, I will get over it. I always do.
• My parents will never get over this! I can't stand this!	• The truth is: my parents may be upset, but they will get over this. I can stand this; I can deal with this.
• Failing a test proves that I am stupid.	• Failing a test means that I failed a test. This does not prove I am stupid.

A Few Coach's Notes on Sensible Thinking

In working with young people, we need to keep in mind that there is no single, correct substitute for a silly self-statement. As students work through the stories and examples in this program, they will come up with their own substitutes for irrational self-talk – and these are often better that the ones suggested in the program!

It should be understood, too, that the four categories (of silly thinking) are often overlapping. For example, an exaggerated self-statement may well be magical (unproven) as well. A particular negative thought might also be described as quite rigid. It may even be the case that a particular wrong-thinking thought could fit all of the categories of silly thinking.

It is important to remember that using sensible self-talk has the overall purposes of reducing unnecessary stress and promoting emotional confidence – especially in the long term. When students are challenged to come up with a more sensible attitude to a particular rotten event, there may be many suggestions that would be appropriate and workable. Some of these suggestions will have the obvious intention of avoiding exaggeration; others will avoid rigid demands, and others will deliberately steer away from magical thinking or jumping to the wrong conclusions without proof. Some of the self-talk suggested by students will have a great relaxing feature, or a wonderful balanced view on something, or a humorous take on something that might be potentially frustrating. The point is: there are many ways to construct a positive thought to a rotten event: keeping a lid on things, seeing humor, not jumping to the wrong conclusions, coaching one's self to be patient, or to be tolerant for the moment, or forgiving, or courageous. In the end, the best rational thoughts do not come from a list, but from a shared discussion.

Encouraging Young People to Act

It is helpful to understand that our immediate reactions to frustrating events serve a biological purpose: to reduce stress. And, this is true, even when we over-react: a temper tantrum allows the sudden build-up of neurotransmitters in the brain and chemicals in the body to dissipate. Simply put: when I yell at someone, it serves the purpose of reducing my own tension, my own stress. Under-reactions serve the same purpose: when I hide or flee from the problem, a certain amount of panic and stress leaves the body.

The goal of this program is to teach students stress-reducing strategies that are, in the long run, appropriate, successful, practical, and fair. In terms of appropriate reactions, this program endorses action plans that are calm and strong. Implementing a calm, strong action plan is to defuse the emotional brain, to short-circuit the flooding of neurotransmitters (or downshifting) before it happens. It is the conviction of this program that – with a certain amount of work, practice, and encouragement – kids can learn to control their explosive over-reactions and their fear-fighting under-reactions. All kids can learn to act wisely in the face of stressful events.

As discussed, the lessons of this program have a strong emphasis on rethinking rotten events. Students are coached, throughout the lessons, to explore their own beliefs and attitudes in the face of rotten events – and, importantly, to see the critical differences between harmful and helpful self-talk. A strong thrust of this program, for sure, relates to the encouragement of students to trade those rigid, pessimistic, unsuccessful, smothering self-statements for ones that are more flexible, optimistic, successful, liberating.

Yet, there is an equally important message for all kids – and summed up nicely by Norman Vincent Peale: "If you don't act on your problems, you will make fear. So, even if your actions are not perfect – it is better to act. Any action is better than

The goal of this program is to teach students stress-reducing strategies that are, in the long run, appropriate, successful, practical, and fair.

no action at all." Yes, right thinking about the problem is the critical first step, but you will need to do something differently. You need to plan what you will do next – for today perhaps, or tomorrow, or next week, or for the very long haul. It is the antithesis of downshifting – it is the call to act.

In *Discipline with Dignity* (1999) Richard Curwin and Allen Mendler underscore the importance of having kids learn specific social skills: "Don't run. Don't fight. Don't throw food. Most teachers have rules so students know what not to do, but we rarely teach students what to do instead." Yes, if young people are going to improve their ability to manage rotten events, to deal with stressful situations more successfully, they will need to explore and apply workable strategies.

The various lessons in *When Rotten Things Happen* encourage students to explore various actions to take in solving problems, and the result, over the course of the program, is the building of a skills repertoire – a menu of calm, strong options. In some cases the teacher or counselor (facilitating these lessons) will want to contribute some suggestions but, once again, the best ideas often come from students themselves. As Vygotsky makes clear: When kids share and debate, when they are "solving problems that encourage (them) to go beyond their current skill and knowledge level," they are developing their higher functions as learners. In a climate of democracy and encouragement, students will offer smart action plans for problem scenarios and then, as it is helpful, they can discuss and debate these.

Encouraging Students to Make Connections

In his pioneering treatise, *Understanding Human Nature* (1927), Alfred Adler set forth explicit ideas about the nature of all human beings. The first thing to understand, according to Adler, is the fact that we humans are uniquely social beings. To a great extent all of us are motivated by social concerns, and our sense of self-worth is strongly connected to our ability to fit in or find our place in the community. Rudolf Dreikurs, Bernice Grunwald and Floyd Pepper have applied Adler's basic constructs to an understanding of children's misbehavior. In their book for classroom teachers, *Maintaining Sanity in the Classroom* (1971) they highlight Adler's notion that "although the child is born without preparation for the complexity of social living, he is a truly social being." And, "as a social being, each child wants to belong. His behavior indicates the ways and means by which he tries to be significant."

It is the fundamental realization that people need people, and it greatly benefits all young people to be involved in supportive, trusting relationships. That does not mean that young people should strive to be liked by everybody around them – in fact, the frenetic desire to be popular is most likely connected to rigid, exaggerated silly beliefs and is often the source of a great deal of adolescent angst. Still, at least one trusting relationship is a very significant thing for any young person – and a legitimate need.

Dr. Mel Levine (2001) observes that "many anxious children improve dramatically when they feel school is a safe place," and further, "children who are anxious need to know that there is at least one person in school in whom they can confide their concerns." This is consistent with the observations of Bonnie Benard (1991) in her long-time work with kids who have grown up in very adverse conditions; she points to three key factors that foster a resilience in these kids, despite their awful environment: caring and supportive relationships; positive and high expectations; opportunities for meaningful participation. Regardless of the program we are using with students, it is important to recognize the value in helping young people to actively explore a support network – even if that is one person.

It is obvious that some kids struggle mightily in their attempts to confide with others and the teacher/counselor will have to be sensitive to this. Some students will benefit from some explicit teaching in these skills; they will feel safer and more confident when they have worked out plans for those key issues: When will you approach your Mom? Where will you meet? What will you say? How will you say it? What will you do if things don't go exactly the way you hope? What positive self-talk would help you? In some cases, kids may want to actually rehearse or role-play these meetings.

As previously described, the action plans in *When Rotten Things Happen* direct students to think sensibly about rotten events, and to conceive practical, useful plans to solve problems. And, importantly, each action plan regularly prompts the young person to actively make a connection – to privately confide with someone else about the problem, with a parent perhaps, or a sibling, or a friend, or a coach, or a teacher or counselor. Implicit in having kids make connections is the idea that social isolation is not especially desirable or healthy. That said, there are two caveats to this part of the plan: First, students need to be reminded that their connections should be restricted to people whom they know and trust. Second, there are some students who manifest learning or emotional conditions that make it very unlikely that they would initiate a connection on their own; your own discretion and sensitivity – and perhaps help – are important here.

The SAT-Plan

The Sensible Acting and Thinking (SAT) Plan provides a simple, compact framework for students to use in the face of rotten events. The SAT Plan is the antithesis of over-and-under reactions. In essence, it is the calm, strong alternative and it incorporates the best principles emotional education, prompting and encouraging students to:

- Defuse the impulsive emotional brain and activate the thinking brain"

- Deliberately avoid over-reacting to rotten events

- Question – and actively refute – silly self-talk based on thinking that may be exaggerated, rigid, negative or magical (unproven)

> **The Sensible Acting and Thinking (SAT) Plan provides a simple, compact framework for students to use in the face of rotten events.**

- Explore – and trust – sensible self-talk based on thinking that is balanced, flexible, positive or empirical

- Recognize the futility and harmfulness of over-and-under reactions and to actively refute these as options for reducing personal stress

- Explore and select calm, strong, appropriate action plans that are ultimately more responsible and successful

- See the benefit of confiding in others about difficult problems, and (where it is helpful and practical) invite personal connections into their own lives – from another young person or a trusted adult

- Reflect on their own attempts to use the SAT Plan, to review what might need changing and, importantly, to privately celebrate one's efforts to be a responsible problem solver

The 4-part SAT Plan uses specific prompts to help students control their own emotions and their subsequent actions. The following is a first-person explanation:

	I tell myself to STOP. RELAX. The first step in the SAT Plan is the most critical. In the face of a rotten event I am paying attention to my own body, to my emerging emotions, and to my dangerous, exaggerated self-talk. By telling myself to stop, relax I am defusing my emotional brain and triggering my thinking brain. I am controlling my emotions.
	I tell myself to THINK SENSIBLY. BE STRONG. BE CALM. I am coaching myself to stay strong and calm. I know that exaggerated, rigid, negative or magical self-talk will spike an under-reaction or an over-reaction. I try to stop these thoughts and to start thinking more positively and sensibly about the rotten thing that has happened.
	I tell myself to MAKE A PLAN. What can I do to make this rotten thing less rotten? What can I do to improve the situation? I need to think of a calm, strong, intelligent, workable plan. I cannot always make things perfect but can always try to make things better.
	I tell myself to MAKE A CONNECTION. Whom should I talk to about this difficulty? I try to think of someone I know and trust: one of my parents perhaps, or a friend, or my teacher or counselor. It feels good just to talk about the situation, to be supported – and, too, I might get some helpful advice.

A Sensible Thinking Primer – Coaching Kids to Coach Themselves

To sum it all up: *When Rotten Things Happen* is a set of exercises that helps students help themselves. The essential life messages are these: think sensibly about those rotten things that happen to you; always support yourself; be your own best friend; be hopeful; have patience, be brave; take risks.

In essence, we (teachers, counselors) are encouraging young people to coach themselves through the unpredictability and turmoil that is, at least sometimes, part of life. We are suggesting to young people that it is far better to be a wise, positive, forever-supportive self-coach than it is to be a silly-thinking, stiff, berating self-coach. And, it is through their own self-talk that they can learn to be their own best coaches. Please see Appendix 2. (This self coaching primer might be reproduced for the students, or it might be magnified and displayed in the room). The far better primer states:

1. **I am unique. I am good.**

   I am living in a very material world, where advertisements on television and magazines are constantly telling all of us to buy more and more things, and to constantly compare ourselves to others. In our society, there is often a lot of pressure to have more stuff in order to fit in, to be popular. This is a dangerous life-attitude. When I constantly compare myself to others, I will always feel unworthy. After all, there will always be people who have talents I do not have, or who have more money, or who look better, or who are more popular.

I will coach myself to have a healthy, positive life-attitude. I will remember that we are not what we own. Each of us has strengths and weaknesses. I will not compare myself to others. I am who I am. I am a unique person in the world. I am not perfect – but I am good. This is a far better life-attitude.

2 Life isn't fair. Get over it. Move on.

Rotten things sometimes happen. People sometimes do rotten things. Life is sometimes less than fair. That's just the way it is. When I demand that the world should always be fair, or when I tell myself over and over that people should be fair all the time, I will always feel helpless and frustrated. This can be very stressful.

It is far better to coach myself that rotten things sometimes happen, that life is not always fair, that people are not always fair. I can accept that, get over it, and move on.

3. Be calm. Be strong.

I know that when a rotten thing happens, I always have a choice. I can choose to yell and scream and threaten and fight – but such over-reactions almost always make the rotten thing more rotten. I can withdraw from people and sulk and do nothing – but such under-reactions never make the rotten thing less rotten. Or, I can choose to act calmly and strongly.

When something rotten happens, it is far better to coach myself to be calm and strong. If I can stick up for myself and take action in a way that shows coolness and strength, things always turn out better.

4. Don't hate. Always forgive.

I can certainly choose to hate people when they are rotten to me. I can try to get back at them and try to make them feel bad – just like they made me feel bad. But hate only piles up, and getting back at others never really teaches them a lesson at all – it only makes them hate me more and it makes them want to get back at me all the more. Worse than that, is the fact that hating others is very heavy, very draining, very stressful.

Refusing to hate is a brave choice. Forgiveness is a brave choice. When I coach myself to forgive, I am breaking the never-ending cycle of hate. It is far better, far less stressful, to walk the halls with a feeling of peace and forgiveness than to walk the halls with hatred and feelings of revenge.

5. Be patient. This will pass.

When a rotten thing happens, it seems to fill me up like water fills a sponge. I often think that this will be rotten forever, or I will be sad about this for a long, long time. These thoughts can be very stressful, and they might very well cause me to panic.

When I feel completely swallowed up by some rotten happening, it is helpful to coach myself to be patient, to remind myself that this rotten thing will pass. I need to remember that time heals all wounds – it really does. Don't panic, be patient – this is far better.

6. Find a quite space. Breathe deeply.

It is sometimes very difficult to be myself. There are times when my living space is very busy, very hectic, very stressful – and during these times it becomes very difficult to think calmly and to make my own decisions.

When I feel that my world is becoming too busy and stressful, I will coach myself to look for a quiet space, where I can calm down, think sensibly, and breathe deeply. I know that it is not always possible for me to leave an uncomfortable place, but whenever I can go to a place that is peaceful and quiet, I am able to relax my whole body, breathe deeply, be myself – and that is far better.

7. **Don't jump to conclusions. Don't assume the worst.**

When I am not included in a conversation, I may be tempted to think the worst – that people don't really like me. If I am not hired for the job I wanted, I might think that no one will ever hire me. If I fail a math test, I might think that I am stupid. Such conclusions are unproven, gloomy, and self-hurting. When I jump to conclusions, and assume the worst, I am setting myself up for sadness.

Whenever I feel rejected, I will coach myself to stay confident, stay positive. I will ask myself: What does this really mean? What does this really prove? Jumping to conclusions is dangerous and self-defeating. It is far better to think sensibly and assume the best.

8. **Lighten up. It's not the end of the world.**

I may have a tendency to – at least sometimes – awfulize or horriblize or terriblize some rotten thing that has happened to me. If I tell myself that a rotten event is truly awful, horrible, terrible, then it becomes that – and I am then likely to feel tremendous sadness, anger or frustration. My own horriblizing self-talk has the power to make a rotten happening a lot more rotten.

In the face of a rotten event, I will coach myself to stop awfulizing – and, instead, to lighten up. It helps to remind myself that most things are not awful-horrible-terrible – they are only unfortunate or annoying, or a little troubling. It helps, also, to remind myself that most rotten things are not the end of the world. I can teach myself to lighten up or to see some humor in it - and that is far better.

9. **Work to change those things that can be changed. Don't sweat those things that cannot be changed.**

It is possible to get bogged down about things that seem rotten. I might become very frustrated about the amount of noise in my neighborhood, or about how tall or short I happen to be, or about my parents divorce – things that I really cannot change. When I constantly fret about these unchangeable things, my life can be very stressful.

It makes sense to try to change those things that I can change, especially when they will lead to my overall happiness. But, clearly, there are things that I really cannot hope to change. I can coach myself not to worry about those things that I don't have much chance of changing. I will actively refuse to worry about those unchangeable things – and that is far better.

10. **Do not fear failure. Take a chance. Go for it!**

I may want to pass on opportunities that would actually help me to grow or to add to my happiness – especially when those opportunities risk failure. I might think that if I don't try out for the team, I won't risk failing to make the team; if I don't perform the guitar solo in front of an audience, I don't risk them laughing at me. It is very tempting to stay in my comfort zone, to not take chances, to not risk failing.

When something is important to me, I will coach myself to move out of my comfort zone. I will take a risk – especially when the risk involves my personal growth and happiness. I will not be afraid of failure. I will congratulate myself for having the courage to take a chance – and that is far better.

When Rotten Things Happen – A Summary of the Key Objectives

When Rotten Things Happen is a program of emotional wellness for pre-and-young adolescents. The simplest, broadest aim behind the lessons of this program is this: To help young people act wisely in the face of those unfortunate experiences, big and not so big, which are part and parcel of life, of growing up.

To that end, and within the context of the 40 lessons, there are 10 key objectives:

1. To create a safe, caring space where students will choose to support each other.

2. To promote in students a deeper awareness of their emotional selves.

3. To help students understand the relationship between their own self-talk and their reactions to those rotten things that happen.

4. To teach students to clearly distinguish among over-reactions, under-reactions, and appropriate reactions.

5. To encourage students, in the face of a rotten event, to purposely avoid over-reactions and under-reactions and to actively choose appropriate reactions.

6. To empower students in their personal stress management by teaching them the SAT Plan – a sensible alternative to under-and-over reacting.

7. To discourage social isolation and aloofness (when dealing with a stressful event) and, alternatively, to encourage connectedness, and open, honest communication (with other known, trusted individuals).

8. To build character development by naming and celebrating the virtues of courage, patience, fairness, empathy, forgiveness and tolerance.

9. To create opportunities for students to share ideas in sensible acting and thinking.

10. To prompt students to actively generalize the skills and ideas (from these lessons) to their everyday lives

Rotten Things Happen

NEGATIVE THINKING

Self-Talk that is...

Exaggerated

Unproven

Negative

Rigid

PROBLEM HAS NO RESOLUTION

No real, long-term improvement

No real emotional growth

OVER-REACTION

Overly emotional

Too hard

Acting Out

A fight response

OR

UNDER-REACTION

Overly emotional

Too timid

Withdrawing

A flight response

SENSIBLE THINKING
Self-Talk that is...

Balanced

Proven

Positive

Flexible

PROBLEM HAS RESOLUTION

Long-term improvement

Emotional Growth

APPROPRIATE REACTION based on...

Calm, strong response

A thoughtful plan

A connection – with a parent, friend, teacher, counselor...

Ready, Set, Go!

Counselor, teacher, youth leader, before launching this program, you need to consider well what you are doing, or as the Boy Scouts are fond of saying, be prepared. Take some time to set your personal goals and reflect on all of the logistics that are involved in presenting these lessons. You should get yourself ready – by fully understanding the program, get yourself set – by making necessary decisions about the group, time and place, and then you are ready to go – by creating and monitoring a safe, supportive learning environment!

Get Ready: Understand the Program

The first direction in terms of getting ready to deliver this program is to browse through the lessons. This preview will add to your understanding, and you will notice some important features and characteristics of the entire program. Among them:

There are 40 lessons addressing 5 areas of rotten things that are potentially stressful for young people: Pressures; Unfairness; Conflicts; Failures and Unexpected Things; Fears and Nightmares.

Each lesson has 4 parts, 4 pages:

First page: The Lesson Plan – is essentially a plan for the teacher/counselor to follow. Each lesson plan follows the same format including an introduction, a scenario, a practice and share session using the SAT plan and a follow-up journal writing exercise.

Second page: When Emotions Take Over – is framed as a social story for the students and teacher/counselor to read and discuss together. It introduces a character facing a rotten event and illustrates how her/his negative/dire/exaggerated/rigid self-talk ignites the character's Emotional Brain, leading to an under-reaction (to the rotten event) or to an over-reaction.

Third page: Using the SAT Plan – is likewise for students and teacher/counselor to read discuss together, this page develops the social story to its essential message: how the character's calm, sensible self-talk contributes to an appropriate reaction; the rotten event becomes less rotten; stress, anxiety, anger, frustration are thereby diminished or deleted. In each social story the character uses the SAT (Sensible Acting Thinking) Plan to engage his/her Thinking Brain; the SAT-Plan becomes the model, the vehicle, that guides individuals to calm, strong responses to rotten events in life.

Before you begin, consider well; and when you have considered, act.
- Sallust (86 – 34 B.C.)

Fourth page: Practice and Share – is essentially an application exercise; the student is prompted (by the teacher/counselor) to independently create a SAT-Plan by inventing a similar scenario and then, through drawing and writing, showing that a character responding calmly and strongly to that rotten event.

Altogether, the lessons have one fundamental idea: when faced with a stressful, rotten event, a character has 3 options: to over-react (by acting out), to under-react (by dropping out), or to react appropriately. Further to this idea: over-and-under reactions are directly related to silly (negative and irrational) thinking and desperate, unsuccessful actions, whereas appropriate reactions are directly related to sensible (positive and rational) thinking and appropriate, successful actions.

Students learn the cognitive and behavioral strategies to effectively mange the stress of rotten things by the deliberate repetition of language and key concepts: over-reaction; under-reaction; appropriate reaction; silly self-talk; sensible self-talk; making connections; the SAT-Plan.

Get Set: Decide on the Group, the Time and the Place

Who will benefit from this program? The short answer is: any one. Once again, *When Rotten Things Happen* is a program of universal wellness – built on the principles of sensible thinking and responsible acting; it is a program of enablement – emphasizing personal accountability and helping young people to help themselves.

As such, this might be instituted as a course in emotional education for an entire classroom, grade level, or division. The lessons relate very positively to the broader curriculum of social skills instruction or basic mental hygiene. Doing so, is to implement a very significant preventative initiative for students at school: When all kids learn the cognitive and behavioral strategies for managing rotten things, many problems are prevented in the first place. And, when teachers, students (and parents) use familiar concepts regarding behavior, a common language, there is a clarity and sensibility around the issues of discipline.

How to Use This Program

In some instances, *When Rotten Things Happen* will be used as an effective intervention for a targeted group – kids who have obvious needs in the area of behavior self-management and impulse control. With difficult or troubled individuals there are a couple of suggestions: the smaller the group the better; and, structure and consistency will be especially critical.

And, yes, it is quite possible to engage one student in these lessons; this would be a unique, interesting project, but very viable. With a single student, the program might be run as an individual counseling type of venture.

Where will the meetings take place? As best you can, make sure that the space is safe, comfortable and inviting. With small or large groups, you should be strategic about seating arrangements, entry and leaving. Anticipating difficulties allows you to plan for these and to be proactive.

When will the meetings take place? Make sure that the students know the schedule – and stick to it; don't let sessions get missed. How often will you meet? (Suggestion: once or twice a week).

To get set, then, is to be clear about your participant audience, whether that is many, a few, or one. This will help you to establish your own goals for these kids and to be well prepared. As well, you should devise and communicate a clear plan about the time and place for these sessions. In this sense, you are approaching your teaching or counseling in a business-like manner and, in the long run, this is a good thing: routines and consistency, as every teacher knows, prevent many problems.

Go – and Make it Work

Making the experience work will invariably depend on many things – and especially the nature of your group – but, nonetheless, there are some key suggestions here that should be helpful:

- Keep in mind that these lessons are essentially guided practice in helping students manage rotten things; work alongside the children (or child); be a leader but also a learner.

- As a leader, strive to be organized, consistent, fair and honest. Strive not to be sarcastic or judgmental.

- Be less didactic, more democratic.

- It is important to build a positive space for the lessons. Jeanne Gibbs (2006) points to three characteristics that are found in positive spaces: caring and supportive relationships; positive and high expectations; opportunities for meaningful participation.

- Set – and reinforce – a few, simple, clear agreements that will promote a safe, comfortable, supportive place for learning, sharing and turn taking. At the beginning of the program, you should discuss with students the following Our Learning Space Creed (see Appendix 1).

> **Every teacher, every youth worker, knows that a positive, respectful learning space is absolutely critical to any learning or growth that is going to happen.**

- Every teacher, every youth worker, knows that a positive, respectful learning space is absolutely critical to any learning or growth that is going to happen. To that end, you will want to have some early discussion about the Learning Space Creed: What would these rules or agreements look and sound like in this learning space? What might be said or done that would break these agreements? Or, students may wish to add-to or modify this creed in some way. Once these credos are established, it is a good idea to post them; as a group leader your role is to consistently remind students of their eminence and, ideally, the students will come to remind each other.

- In terms of the lessons, provide encouragement and (as appropriate) specific feedback; prompt all students to offer honest thoughts and suggestions relative to these.

- Find a way to encourage sharing. In a sharing atmosphere kids will learn the sensible self-talk and successful actions that have worked for others.

- On occasion you may want to model some of the concepts or strategies or self-talk associated with the lessons.

- Monitor each student's success; help the student gain a sense of how I am doing in this project.

- Finally – and importantly - explore ways to get young people to use the strategies and ideas of this program outside the classroom. Encourage them to generalize what they are learning by using the language of the program in the day-to-day issues with young people, by inviting them to share stories of how they used some of the strategies, and, simply, by telling them to generalize.

Once you are ready, once you are set – then go! Good luck and good teaching with this dynamic program for young people!

When Rotten Things Happen

The Lessons

All over the place, from the popular culture to the propaganda system, there is constant pressure to make people feel that they are helpless, that the only role they can have is to ratify decisions and to consume.
- Noam Chomsky

Lesson One:
The Pressure to Fit in at School

Ⓐ INTRODUCTION

The Social Story in Lesson One is about Sammy. He is feeling a lot of pressure to fit in at his school – to have stylish clothes to wear, and to show up with the latest cell phone and other electronic gadgets that other kids are taking to school.

Lesson One shows how Sammy's own negative thinking about not having the clothes and gadgets to fit in is causing feelings of anger and resentment towards others.

Ⓑ THE SCENARIO

1. Do a Guided/Shared Reading of Pressure to Fit-in at School: When Emotions Take Over

   Create a Discussion about Sammy's situation, his feelings, his reactions:
   • How would you describe Sammy's feelings in this story?
   • What do you think were causing these (angry) feelings?

2. Now do a Guided/Shared Reading using the S.A.T. Plan.
   Create a Discussion about Sammy's reaction this time:
   • How was Sammy able to think differently about the rotten event (of not fitting in)?
   • How did his feelings (or emotions) change?
   • How was his behavior (what he did) this time different?

3. Have students complete the practice page on this topic, and share their ideas with 2 or 3 others.

Ⓒ FOLLOW-UP

Suggested prompts for Journal Writing:
• What was important to you about Sammy's story?
• What personal connections can you make to the story?
• Did you find the lesson meaningful in any way? Why? Why not?

If I don't get some better clothes, my classmates will think I'm a loser!

SCENARIO

There is pressure for Sammy to fit in at school. Part of this fitting in is to have as much as other kids in his class – have the nicest clothes, the latest computer, the coolest cell phone, and the newest music devices. Yes, fitting in can be expensive, and Sammy knows that his family does not have money to blow.

NEGATIVE THINKING

When Sammy thinks he is not fitting in at school, his brain is often flooded with negative thoughts. "I **need** to have my friends respect me."

"If I don't dress well, **they will think I'm a nerd**. My friends **won't like me**."

"I **can't stand it** when I can't buy the things I need in order to fit in at school."

"I must be a **loser**."

EMOTIONS TAKE OVER

Sammy's negative thoughts bring negative emotions. He sometimes feels **worthless** and **unlikeable**. He sometimes feels **anger** towards his parents for not giving him the enough money to fit in at school. He sometimes **hates** kids who have more than he is able to have.

There are days when he **hates** the world.

THE UNDER–REACTION

Perhaps he should keep to himself or just stay home from school.

THE OVER–REACTION

Perhaps he should be sassy to his parents and sarcastic to his classmates – especially those who have more than he does. That would show them all!

Nice threads Nicky boy. Did you get them at the dog pound?

IN THE END...Sammy has not helped himself.

Staying home from school is like the ostrich hiding its head in the sand – the problems have not gone away. Becoming sassy with his parents will only make his home life worse. Becoming sarcastic with friends and classmates will only make him less popular.

Keeping to himself and staying home from school are **UNDER-REACTIONS.** The problem just gets bigger.
Being sassy and being sarcastic are **OVER-REACTIONS**. The problem just gets bigger.

Using the S.A.T. Plan – The Pressure to Fit in at School

Needing to fit in'.... I'm going to start thinking about this differently.

Sammy decides to look at ways that will make his problem smaller. He wants to feel better about himself. He wants to deal with his feelings of not fitting in at school in more positive ways. He wants to decrease his feelings of being disliked and increase his feelings of confidence at school.

Sammy uses the 4- part SAT (Sensible Acting & Thinking) Plan.

STOP. RELAX.

Sammy monitors his own feelings. When he begins to feel rotten about not fitting in, he immediately tells himself, **"Stop. Relax. Cool down. Stop thinking that way!"**

He may need to do this when a classmate says something, or when he sees someone wearing new clothes, or when he thinks that people are ignoring him, or when someone makes a snide comment.

THINK SENSIBLY. BE CALM. BE STRONG.

Sammy starts to challenge the truth in his negative self-talk. He changes negative self-talk to positive self-talk.

THE TRUTH IS...

"My friends won't disown me if I don't have as much as they do."

"I don't have to have things in order to fit in at school."

"I don't have to fit in all the time, anyway."

"Sometimes kids are just insensitive – I can deal with that. I can be calm and strong."

MAKE A PLAN

I'm going to wear what I want - not what others want me to wear. I'm going to stop all my negative thinking about this.

MAKE A CONNECTION

Sammy has a chat with his buddy, Juan. They have a good talk about all the pressures of fitting into the group at school. Sammy finds out that Juan often feels the same way.

IN THE END...Sammy has helped himself.

When something happens at school to trigger his feelings of not fitting in, he **stops himself**. He changes his negative self-talk into **positive self-talk**. He reminds himself that friends are important, yes, but needing to "fit" through clothes and things and money is a dead-end street.

Now, he acts differently. When he starts to become sassy with his parents or sarcastic with friends he stops himself. He learns to **fit in on his own terms**, and he makes an **important connection** – this time with a buddy. Slowly, steadily, he is becoming **more confident**.

My Picture	What has happened? **OR** What might happen?

STOP. RELAX. What other self-talk could help me **avoid over-reacting** to a feeling of not fitting in at school?	**THINK SENSIBLY. BE CALM. BE STRONG.** What other **positive self-talk** could help me think sensibly about this?

MAKE A PLAN	**MAKE A CONNECTION**

IN THE END...What is Likely to Happen?
Be honest. Be realistic.

Lesson Two:
Pressures at Home

Ⓐ INTRODUCTION

The Social Story in Lesson Two is about Dina. She is feeling a lot of pressure at her home – specifically, to have the respect and confidence of her mom.

Lesson Two shows how Dina's exaggerated self-talk about the pressures she if facing at home is causing feelings of hatred towards her own mother.

Ⓑ THE SCENARIO

1. Do a Guided/Shared Reading of Pressures at Home: When Emotions Take Over.
   Create a Discussion about Dina's situation, her feelings, her reactions:
   • Why do you think Dina was becoming too hateful towards her mother?
   • How is an under-reaction different from an over-reaction?

2. Now do a Guided/Shared Reading using the S.A.T. Plan.
   Create a Discussion about Dina's reaction this time:
   • How has Dina's self-talk changed (from the earlier scenario)?
   • How did this self-talk make her feel (this time)?
   • How did the new self-talk change her actions towards her mother?

3. Have students complete the practice page on this topic, and share their ideas with 2 or 3 others.

Ⓒ FOLLOW-UP

Suggested prompts for Journal Writing:
• What might be a life lesson from Dina's story?
• What personal connections can you make to the story?
• Did you find the lesson meaningful in any way? Why? Why not?

My home... my Mom.... pressure, pressure, pressure!

SCENARIO 2

There are pressures for Dina at home. Part of this pressure is to follow the rules of the house. Sometimes Dina's Mom gets angry at her for not doing enough chores around the house – like cleaning her room and making dinner. It seems to Dina that her Mom favors, Dina's sister, Nell. Dina feels a lot of pressure trying to fit in at home.

NEGATIVE THINKING

When Dina thinks she is not fitting in at home, her brain is often filled with negative thoughts.

"I **need** to have my mom respect me."

"If I don't do everything she wants around the house, **she will think I'm letting down the family. She will hate me.**"

"**I know my mom likes my sister better than me.**"

"As a daughter, I am a **loser.**"

EMOTIONS TAKE OVER

Dina's negative thoughts bring negative emotions. Around home she feels **like she does not belong**. She sometimes feels **anger** towards her mom for putting so much pressure on her.

There are days when she **hates** her mom, her sister and the whole world.

THE UNDER-REACTION

Perhaps Dina should come home every night, go up to her room, and not talk to anyone. She might just mope and sulk the whole year round.

THE OVER-REACTION

Perhaps Dina could throw a tantrum every time her mom nagged at her. Perhaps she should throw something at her goody-goody sister. That would teach them both a lesson!

IN THE END...Dina has not helped herself.

Moping and sulking will not help her mom to understand her feelings, and throwing temper tantrums will only make the house noisier.

Depending on what Dina does, her problem becomes bigger or smaller.

Moping in her room is an **UNDER-REACTION**. The problem just gets bigger.

Yelling and screaming and throwing things are **OVER-REACTIONS**. The problem just gets bigger.

Using the S.A.T. Plan – Pressures at Home

> Every problem is like a balloon. Depending on what I do, it gets bigger or it gets smaller.

Dina decides to let some air out of the balloon – to find ways that will make her problem smaller. She knows that she feels insecure at home, but she also knows that moping and yelling do not help. She wants to lessen those rotten feelings.

Dina uses the 4- part SAT (Sensible Acting & Thinking) Plan.

 STOP. RELAX.

Dina tries to become more aware of her own feelings. When she begins to feel bad about not fitting in, she right away tells herself, **"Stop. Relax. Count to ten."**

Dina realizes that she sometimes needs to walk away from her mom or her sister. When she does this, she will say: "I need to take a break. I will be back." Dina knows that it is better to talk about hot issues **after she has cooled down.**

 THINK SENSIBLY. BE CALM. BE STRONG.

Dina starts to realize that it is her **negative thoughts** that are triggering her feelings of insecurity at home. She works at changing **negative thinking to positive thinking**.

THE TRUTH IS...

"My mom loves me. I need to **remember** that."

"I don't have to **be like my sister** in order to **fit in** at home."

"Yes, sometimes there is a little pressure at home – but **I can deal with that**. I can be calm and strong."

 MAKE A PLAN

> STOP. Relax. Breathe deeply. Take a break. Talk it over when I cool down.

 MAKE A CONNECTION

> Mom, can we have a quiet talk about something?

IN THE END...Dina has helped herself.

When her mom or sister says something to spark feelings of not fitting in, she stops herself. She examines her negative self-talk and realizes that most of it is **not true**. She does not allow her brain to reach the wrong conclusions: **Just because her mom gets on her case about school doesn't mean her mom does not love her or respect her.** In these discussions, Dina is able to stay calm, stay cool.

Dina also tries to act differently. When she starts to become angry with her mom or her sister, she **stops herself**. She learns to fit in on her own terms, and she makes a **meaningful connection** – especially with her mom. Little by little she is becoming **more relaxed, less worried**.

My Picture	What has happened? **OR** What might happen?
STOP. RELAX. What other self-talk could help me **avoid over-reacting** to pressures at home?	**THINK SENSIBLY. BE CALM. BE STRONG.** What other **positive self-talk** could help me think sensibly' about this?
MAKE A PLAN	**MAKE A CONNECTION**

IN THE END...What is Likely to Happen?
Be honest. Be realistic.

Lesson Three:
Pressure to do Well Academically

Ⓐ INTRODUCTION

The Social Story in Lesson Three is about Tyrone. He is feeling a lot of pressure to do well academically – to get good grades and still have an enjoyable social life.

Lesson Three shows how Tyrone's negative, unproven ideas about not doing well in school are causing general feelings of resentment.

Ⓑ THE SCENARIO

1. Do a Guided/Shared Reading of Pressure to Do Well Academically: When Emotions Take Over.
   Create a Discussion about Tyrone's situation, his feelings, his reactions:
   • Why would Tyrone decide to simply give up on school?
   • Re-read Tyrone's self-talk. How much of this self-talk was unproven?

2. Now do a Guided/Shared Reading using the S.A.T. Plan.
   Create a Discussion about Tyrone's reaction this time:
   • How has Tyrone's self-talk changed (from the earlier scenario)?
   • How did this self-talk become more sensible, more logical?
   • How did the new self-talk change his actions?

3. Have students complete the practice page on this topic, and share their ideas with 2 or 3 others.

Ⓒ FOLLOW-UP

Suggested prompts for Journal Writing:
• What do you think is the important lesson in Tyrone's story?
• What personal connections can you make to the story?
• How difficult do you think it is to change our self-talk about rotten things that happen to us?

SCENARIO 3

There is pressure for Tyrone to do well at school. There is homework almost every night and there are tests every week. There are times when Tyrone gets bogged down with all of these school pressures. He knows that school is important but he also wants to have some time in his life to do other things. Sometimes Tyrone hates school!

NEGATIVE THINKING

When Tyrone thinks about all of the pressures of school, his thoughts become negative.

"I **can't stand** all of these school pressures. School is **killing me**."

"If I don't do well in school, it proves I am **stupid**."

"Those good students make me feel like a **loser**."

EMOTIONS TAKE OVER

Tyrone's negative thoughts are tied to very negative emotions. He often feels **stupid** and **inferior to other** students. The feelings of worthlessness trigger feelings of **anger and hatred**. There are days when he **totally hates** school, those good students in school – and even his parents.

THE UNDER–REACTION

Perhaps Tyrone should just give up on school. That would get rid of all the pressures of school.

That's it! I give up!

TRASH

THE OVER-REACTION

Perhaps Tyrone could bully other kids – especially the ones who were plugged into school. He would get respect by having others be afraid of him!

Hey kid....

IN THE END...Tyrone has not helped himself.

Giving up on school will only put a different kind of pressure on him – the real-life pressures of having to get a job and support himself. Becoming a bully creates other pressures as well – the pressure to act tough every day. These plans lead nowhere

Giving up on school is an **UNDER-REACTION.** The pressures of school are still there.
Becoming a hateful, angry bully is an **OVER-REACTION.** The pressures of school are still there.

Using the S.A.T. Plan – Pressure to Do Well Academically

I'm going to make a new path for myself.

Tyrone decides to make some changes that will make his problem smaller. He knows that he feels pressure about school, but he also knows that giving up on school does not help. Tyrone wants to lessen those rotten feelings.

Tyrone uses the 4- part SAT (Sensible Acting & Thinking) Plan.

 ## STOP. RELAX.

Tyrone starts to pay more attention to his own feelings. When he begins to feel bad about school pressures, he tells himself, **"Stop. Relax. Don't overreact."**

Tyrone learns to bite his tongue – he stops himself from saying negative, hurtful things. When he is able to cool down, take a deep breath, **he actually feels stronger.** He is controlling his emotions – the emotions are not controlling him!

 ## THINK SENSIBLY. BE CALM. BE STRONG.

Tyrone starts to check his own negative thinking. He works at changing negative thinking to positive thinking.

THE TRUTH IS...

"School does not upset me. My **negative thinking upsets me**."

"If I don't do well in school, **it does not mean I am stupid** – not at all."

"Yes, school can be tough – but I can learn to deal with that. I can be **calm** and **strong**."

 ## MAKE A PLAN

I am smart and capable – even if I mess up on a test!

 ## MAKE A CONNECTION

Tyrone touches base with a teacher. He knows that it helps to talk to someone who listens and cares.

IN THE END...Tyrone has helped himself.

Tests and homework may trigger some panic – but Tyrone **stops himself**. He checks his own negative self-talk and realizes that most of it is not true. He does not allow **negative thinking** and **negative emotions** to control him. He reminds himself: **"If I happen not to do well on something at school, it does not mean I am stupid. I don't need to be afraid of school."** These self-reminders help Tyrone to stay calm, stay cool.

Tyrone also tries to act differently. He actively refuses to give up on school. He makes some important changes in his life – around homework and studying. And, makes an important connection – with a teacher who is willing to help him with his plan. Change is hard, but week by week, Tyrone is becoming less uptight, more confident about school. **Tyrone is learning to manage his own stress.**

My Picture	What has happened? **OR** What might happen?
STOP. RELAX. What other self-talk could help me **avoid over-reacting** to the pressures at school?	**THINK SENSIBLY. BE CALM. BE STRONG.** What other **positive self-talk** could help me think sensibly' about this?
MAKE A PLAN	**MAKE A CONNECTION**

IN THE END...What is Likely to Happen?
Be honest. Be realistic.

Lesson Four:
Getting a Job

Ⓐ INTRODUCTION

The Social Story in Lesson Four is about Lindsay. She is feeling a lot of pressure to get a job, to make some money in order to buy several things that she wants.

Lesson Four shows how Lindsay's exaggerated thoughts about absolutely needing money are causing feelings of over-anxiety for her.

Ⓑ THE SCENARIO

1. Do a Guided/Shared Reading of Getting a Job: When Emotions Take Over.
    Create a Discussion about Lindsay's situation, her feelings, her reactions:
    • Examine Lindsay's self-talk. How would you describe it?
    • Why would Lindsay's "I need" statements cause such anxiety for her?

2. Now do a Guided/Shared Reading using the S.A.T. Plan.
    Create a Discussion about Lindsay's reaction this time:
    • How would you describe Lindsay's new self-talk?
    • How would this more logical self-talk cause her to act differently to her problem?
    • How did the new self-talk change her life-plans?

3. Have students complete the practice page on this topic, and share their ideas with 2 or 3 others.

Ⓒ FOLLOW-UP

Suggested prompts for Journal Writing:
• How did Lindsay's under-reaction make her problem bigger?
• How did Lindsay's over-reaction make her problem bigger?
• How did Lindsay's appropriate-reaction make her problem smaller?

When Emotions Take Over – Getting a Job

SCENARIO 4

There is pressure for Lindsay to make some money. She could really do with a job! But jobs are tough to get – especially for a young teen. She has asked a number of people on her street, but no luck. Sometimes Lindsay gets depressed when she thinks about all of the things she would like to buy – and she cannot find a job to make any money.

NEGATIVE THINKING

When Lindsay thinks about all of the money pressures, her thoughts become gloomy.

"I **absolutely need** a job so I can buy all the things I want to buy."

"I'll **never find a job.**"

"No one will ever hire me – I'm such a **loser.**"

EMOTIONS TAKE OVER

Lindsay's gloomy thoughts turn into gloomy emotions. When she can't find a job, she blames herself. She then feels **overwhelmed by the world.** She often feels hopeless and she blames herself for not being able to get a job. Lindsay convinces herself that she will never be any good.

THE UNDER–REACTION

Perhaps Lindsay should just give up trying to get a job. That would take all the pressure off of her – and it would also prove, once and for all, that she is not smart or talented enough to get a job.

THE OVER-REACTION

Perhaps Lindsay could blow up at those people who won't give her a job. She could tell them off – that would show them!

IN THE END...Lindsay has not helped herself.

Giving up on a job has not helped her money situation at all. She will still be broke! "Blowing up will only make it more likely that she will not get a job. Giving up and blowing up are plans that will make money problems worse, not better.

Giving up, and not even trying to find a job, is an **UNDER-REACTION.** Her sadness only grows.

Blowing up and telling them off is an **OVER-REACTION.** Her sadness only grows.

Using the S.A.T. Plan – Getting a Job

Lindsay decides to think and act in ways that **make her problem smaller.** She knows that money is important to her right now, but she also knows that giving up and blowing up only make things worse. She wants to **deal with her rotten feelings.**

Lindsay uses the 4- part SAT (Sensible Acting & Thinking) Plan.

 ### STOP. RELAX.

Lindsay starts to get a handle on her own feelings. When she begins to feel depressed about the pressures of money, and not getting a job, she tells herself, **"Stop. Relax. Don't over-react."** Lindsay learns to stop all of the gloomy thoughts that lead to feelings of sadness.

"Calm down, calm down," she tells herself. It's only money. It's not the end of the world."

 ### THINK SENSIBLY. BE CALM. BE STRONG.

Lindsay thinks about her **negative self-talk.** She knows that most of her money **comes from her exaggerated, gloomy self-talk.**

THE TRUTH IS...

"I do not absolutely need money. Yes, I want money and I want a job, but I will be okay, even if I don't get a job right away."

"Things work out. They always do."

"My negative thinking is the real pressure!"

"If I don't get a job, **it does not mean I am stupid or untalented** – just a bit unlucky."

"I can be calm and strong."

 ### MAKE A PLAN

I won't give up!

 ### MAKE A CONNECTION

GUIDANCE

IN THE END...Lindsay has helped herself.

Money problems can be a pressure, yes, but Lindsay stops herself from building up that pressure. She examines her own negative self-talk and realizes that most of it is exaggerated. She does not let her own negative thinking add to her own sadness. Instead, she tells herself: "If I go out and try to get a job, but don't get one, it does not mean that I am stupid or untalented. No, no, no." These **self-encouragements** help Lindsay to take the pressure off of herself.

Lindsay also tries to act positively. She reminds herself to be brave, and not give up trying to find a job. She also makes an important connection – with the school counselor who helps her with a job search. It's not easy, but Lindsay is becoming **braver and more confident. Lindsay is becoming emotionally smart.**

My Picture	What has happened? **OR** What might happen?
STOP. RELAX. What other self-talk could help me **avoid over-reacting** to not finding a job?	**THINK SENSIBLY. BE CALM. BE STRONG.** What other **positive self-talk** could help me think sensibly' about this?
MAKE A PLAN	**MAKE A CONNECTION**

IN THE END...What is Likely to Happen?
Be honest. Be realistic.

Lesson Five:
Smoking

Ⓐ INTRODUCTION

The Social Story in Lesson Five is about Naj. He is feeling a lot of pressure (mainly from his friends) to become a smoker.

Lesson Five shows how Naj's dangerous self-talk about absolutely needing to please his friends is causing him to make unhealthy life-changing decisions.

Ⓑ THE SCENARIO

1. Do a Guided/Shared Reading of Smoking: When Emotions Take Over.
   Create a Discussion about Naj's situation, his feelings, his reactions:
   - How is Naj's self-talk not really sensible or provable?
   - Why are Naj's under-reaction and his over-reaction unwise?

2. Now do a Guided/Shared Reading using the S.A.T. Plan.
   Create a Discussion about Naj's reaction this time:
   - How is Naj's new self-talk more sensible, more truthful?
   - Do you think it would easy for Naj to be as courageous as he wants to be?
   - How would Naj's humor be successful for him?

3. Have students complete the practice page on this topic, and share their ideas with 2 or 3 others.

Ⓒ FOLLOW-UP

Suggested prompts for Journal Writing:
- Do you think that not going along with the group makes your friends really dislike you?
- How difficult is it to act courageously in terms of making your own decisions? Explain.
- What are some ways humor can help in difficult situations – at least sometimes?

SCENARIO 5

There is pressure for Naj to smoke. He hangs out with his buddies after school, and some of them smoke cigarettes. Naj's friends are important to him, but they continually coax him to "have a puff." He feels a lot of pressure to "be like the guys" and to light up like they do. He does not want to smoke, but he often feels torn and confused.

 NEGATIVE THINKING

When Naj thinks about the pressures his buddies put on him his self-talk becomes negative.

"I **need to** have my buddies like me all the time.

"If I don't smoke with them, they won't invite me to be with them after school. I won't have any friends."

"If I don't smoke they will think I'm a **loser.**"

 EMOTIONS TAKE OVER

Naj's negative, unproven self-talk causes harmful emotions. He convinces himself that he **must fit in; he must smoke** in order to be okay. He begins to feel **controlled and threatened by his own friends**. As long as Naj clings to this wrong thinking he will be **greatly bothered** by the pressure to smoke. And – maybe he will give in to that pressure!

 THE UNDER–REACTION

Perhaps Naj should just **give in** to the pressure to smoke. Then, the pressure would be off!

 THE OVER-REACTION

Perhaps Naj should decide not to **hang out with his friends** any more. That would show them!

Sorry dudes.... no time for you guys!

IN THE END...Naj has not helped himself.

Giving in to the pressure will not cause his friends to respect him – it never does! More important, Naj's decision to smoke is unhealthy. Yet, his friends are important to him, and leaving his buddies behind may be an unfortunate thing for him to do.

Giving in to the pressure to smoke is an **UNDER-REACTION** - and much less healthy

Giving up on his important friends is an **OVER-REACTION** – and a lot lonelier.

Using the S.A.T. Plan – Smoking

"No" to smoking, "Yes" to my buddies. Courage is the name of the game!

Naj decides to examine his negative self-talk and to create a plan that will make his problem smaller. His health is important! His self-respect is important! His friends are important. He wants to deal with the pressure to smoke in a positive way.

Naj uses the 4- part SAT (Sensible Acting & Thinking) Plan.

STOP. RELAX.

Naj begins to closely monitor his own feelings. When he begins to feel annoyed and uncomfortable about the pressure to smoke, he tells himself, **"Stop. Relax. Don't overreact."**

Naj learns to stop the unproven, negative thoughts that lead to the uncomfortable feelings.

"Don't get so worked up," he coaches himself. These guys are only teasing.

THINK SENSIBLY. BE CALM. BE STRONG.

Naj thinks more about his **negative self-talk**. He realizes that the real pressure to smoke comes from his own negative thinking.

THE TRUTH IS...

"**I do not need to please** my friends all the time."

"This pressure is only teasing remarks from my buddies. **I can learn to deal with that.** I can learn to be calm and strong."

MAKE A PLAN

1. Don't try to please my friends all the time.
2. Think sensibly about trying to "fit in."
3. Have courage.
4. Be funny....sometimes.

MAKE A CONNECTION

Joey....A lot of the guys are smoking these days....What do you think about that?

IN THE END...Naj has helped himself.

Naj makes up his mind to stand up to the pressure to smoke. The first step is to stop the negative ideas about all the pressure. He works at changing his own unproven, negative self-talk. He realizes that most of the rotten pressure has come from himself. Naj also works at changing what he says and does when his friends tease him. He uses a little humor. And, he makes a connection; he talks about this with a friend.

Naj begins to realize some other things - that friends don't really care if you smoke or not; that a little humor goes a long way; that it is better to be calm and strong than it is to give in or to give up. Day by day Naj is becoming more sensible, more courageous.

My Picture	What has happened? **OR** What might happen?
STOP. RELAX. What other self-talk could help me **avoid over-reacting** to pressure from friends?	**THINK SENSIBLY. BE CALM. BE STRONG.** What other **positive self-talk** could help me think sensibly' about this?
MAKE A PLAN	**MAKE A CONNECTION**

IN THE END...What is Likely to Happen?
Be honest. Be realistic.

Lesson Six:
Taking Drugs

Ⓐ INTRODUCTION

The Social Story in Lesson Six is about Mary. She is feeling a lot of pressure from her peers to drink alcohol, to take drugs.

Lesson Six shows how Mary is conflicted about this pressure – and how positive self-talk will help her to become more of an independent thinker.

Ⓑ THE SCENARIO

1. Do a Guided/Shared Reading of Taking Drugs: When Emotions Take Over.
   Create a Discussion about Mary's situation, her feelings, her reactions:
   • What do you think about Mary's decision to simply cave in to the pressure?
   • What do you think about Mary's decision to name-call and angrily scold her friends?

2. Now do a Guided/Shared Reading using the S.A.T. Plan.
   Create a Discussion about Mary's reaction this time:
   • What do you think about Mary's 4-step plan?
   • She decides to confide in a friend about these pressures. Whom else might she turn to?
   • Do you think Mary will face difficulties or challenges with her new plan?

3. Have students complete the practice page on this topic, and share their ideas with 2 or 3 others.

Ⓒ FOLLOW-UP

Suggested prompts for Journal Writing:
• Write about a time when you decided to act with great courage (about something).
• Write about a time in your life when you decided to be an independent thinker?
• Is it possible to have good friends – but do everything they want you to do? Discuss.

Just saying "no" is not always easy!

SCENARIO 6

There is pressure for Mary to get into drugs. The pressure does not come from strangers or kids on the corner of the street – but from her good friends. For sure, Mary's friends are important to her, but she does not want in any way start to drink or do drugs. At weekend parties, there is a lot of pressure on her. She feels nervous and scared.

NEGATIVE THINKING

When Mary thinks about the pressures to fit in by drinking and experimenting with drugs, her negative self-talk goes into over-drive.

"I **need to** have my friends think I am cool.

"If I don't drink or take drugs, **they will be laughing** at me. I will lose all my friends."

"If I don't get with the drinking and the drugs, they will think I'm a **loser.**"

EMOTIONS TAKE OVER

Mary's dangerous self-talk leads to dangerous emotions. She convinces herself that she **must be cool in front of her friends**; she assumes that she will be **laughed at** for deciding not to drink at a party. She begins to feel **inferior** to her friends – because they do drugs, and she does not. As long as Mary convinces herself that her **friends will disown her,** she thinks she must be a loser.

THE UNDER–REACTION

Perhaps Mary should just cave in to the pressure to party hard – to drink alcohol and to take drugs. Then, the pressure would be gone!

Might as well join the crowd!

THE OVER-REACTION

Perhaps Mary should decide to turn sour on her friends. She could tell them off, every one of them, and tell them all to get lost. They would be sorry!

You guys are a bunch of loooooozers!

IN THE END...Mary has not helped herself.

Caving in to the pressure will not cause her friends to like her more – that never really happens! And, getting into alcohol and drugs could bring even bigger problems for her. Still, her friends are important. They are wrong, but they are important.

Caving in to the pressure to drink or take drugs is an **UNDER-REACTION.** The problem just gets bigger. Turning sour on her friends is an **OVER-REACTION.** The problem just gets bigger.

Using the S.A.T. Plan – Taking Drugs

Mary decides to look closely at her negative self-talk and to do some things that will make her problem smaller. Drugs and alcohol are dangerous – but, still, her friends are special to her. She decides to face-up to the pressure to do drugs in a positive way.

Mary uses the 4- part SAT (Sensible Acting & Thinking) Plan.

 ## STOP. RELAX.

Mary begins to think about her feelings. When she begins to feel foolish and inferior about the pressure to drink, she tells herself, **"Stop. Relax. Don't overreact."**

Mary learns to stop the over-blown, negative thoughts that lead to the feelings of inferiority.

"Don't make wrong assumptions," she tells herself.

 ## THINK SENSIBLY. BE CALM. BE STRONG.

Mary thinks more about her **silly self-talk.** She realizes that her feelings of **nervousness and inferiority** come from her own negative thinking.

THE TRUTH IS...

"I do not need my friends **to approve of everything** I do."

"They might sometimes get on my case, but I can handle that. I can be **calm and strong.**"

MAKE A PLAN

1. Be kind to my friends.
2. Be honest with my friends.
3. Be strong with my friends. AND....
4. Be true to myself!

MAKE A CONNECTION

I hear you Mary.... I can really relate to what you are going through.

IN THE END...Mary has helped herself.

Mary starts to deal with her pressure in a positive way. The first step is to stop the negative thinking about what happens. She starts to change her own dangerous, negative self-talk. She begins to see that most of the rotten pressure has come from herself. Mary starts to change what she says and does with her friends. She **stays strong** – but she **stays calm**. She **makes a connection** with another friend who has similar thoughts about alcohol and drugs.

Mary finds that friends will like you if you are honest and caring – and they don't really care if you drink alcohol or not. Mary stays true to her friends – and to her own values. **Mary is becoming stronger.**

My Picture	What has happened? **OR** What might happen?
STOP. RELAX. What other self-talk could help me **avoid over-reacting** to the pressure to try drugs?	**THINK SENSIBLY. BE CALM. BE STRONG.** What other **positive self-talk** could help me think sensibly' about this?
MAKE A PLAN	**MAKE A CONNECTION**

IN THE END...What is Likely to Happen?
Be honest. Be realistic.

Lesson Seven:
Sex

Ⓐ INTRODUCTION

The Social Story in Lesson Seven is about Brady. She is feeling a lot of social pressure from her peers to become sexually active.

Lesson Seven shows Brady's conflicted thoughts about this pressure – and how positive self-talk will help her to become more of an independent thinker.

Ⓑ THE SCENARIO

1. Do a Guided/Shared Reading of Sex: When Emotions Take Over.
    Create a Discussion about Brady's situation, her feelings, her reactions:
    • What do you think about Brady's decision to simply loosen up to the pressure?
    • What do you think about Brady's decision to spread rumors about some of her friends?

2. Now do a Guided/Shared Reading using the S.A.T. Plan.
    Create a Discussion about Brady's reaction this time:
    • What do you think about Brady's 4-step SAT Plan?
    • How would Brady's SAT-Plan make her problem smaller (in the long run)?
    • Do you think Brady will face difficulties or challenges with her new plan?

3. Have students complete the practice page on this topic, and share their ideas with 2 or 3 others.

Ⓒ FOLLOW-UP

Suggested prompts for Journal Writing:
• Is the pressure to have sex greater for boys or girls? Explain.
• Pretend you have a newspaper column. Write an advice column for Brady's dilemma.
• Pretend you are Brady's best friend. Regarding her pressures, what advice would you give her?

SCENARIO 7

There is pressure for Brady to have sex. Most of the pressure comes from the group she hangs out with – not all of them, but some of them. Brady does not want to be viewed as a goody-goody by her group of friends, yet she wants to operate on her own set of values. She wants to make her own life decisions. She feels confused about what to do.

 NEGATIVE THINKING

When Brady thinks about the pressures to be a risk taker by experimenting with sex, she may have negative thoughts.

"I **must** have my friends like me all the time.

"If I don't take some risks and experiment with sex, **they will all think I am a goody-goody** and they will be gossiping behind my back."

"If I don't start experimenting with sex, they will think I'm a **loser**."

 EMOTIONS TAKE OVER

Brady's rotten self-doubts lead to rotten emotions. She repeatedly tells herself that she **must have her friends approval all the time**. She tells herself that her friends will **laugh at her** for not having sex, as some of them are doing. She begins to feel **less important** to her friends. Brady's unproven, negative ideas lead her to believe that her **friends will never want to be around a goody-goody like her**. Should she do things she does not feel comfortable with in her life right now?

 THE UNDER–REACTION

Well, at least I won't be thought of as a goody-goody.

THE OVER–REACTION

Let me tell you all about Brenda....

IN THE END...Brady has not helped herself

Loosening up to the pressure to have sex will not gain any real respect from her friends. But more important, Brady will be **betraying her own values**. She will be acting out the values of her friends - and that will only make her **more uncomfortable than ever**! Spreading rumors about her friends is a **hostile act** that will only turn the group against her.

Loosening up to the pressure to have sex is an **UNDER-REACTION** – and the problem is still there. Spreading rumors about her friends is an **OVER-REACTION** – and the problem is still there.

Using the S.A.T. Plan – Sex

Brady decides to summon all of her courage – to self-examine her negative thinking and to make some plans that will make her problem smaller. For Brady, sex has many risks – physically and emotionally – but, her group of friends are important to her. She decides to act on her own life values – and no one else's!

Brady sits down and writes a 4- part SAT (Sensible Acting & Thinking) Plan.

 ## STOP. RELAX.

Brady thinks about her emotions. When she begins to feel like a loser about the pressure to have sex, she tells herself, **"Stop. Relax. Don't overreact."**

Brady continually practices stopping the unproven, doubtful thoughts that lead to the feelings of low self-esteem.

"Stop the silly thinking," she tells herself.

 ## THINK SENSIBLY. BE CALM. BE STRONG.

Brady closely examines her silly, negative **self-statements**. She realizes that her feelings of **uncertainty and low self-esteem** come from these negative thoughts.

THE TRUTH IS...

"If I don't do what some of my friends are doing, **that is okay**. I can live with that and my friends can live with that."

"They might sometimes try to persuade me, but I can deal with that. **I act on my own set of values**. I can be a strong friend."

MAKE A PLAN

1. Never do anything because of pressure.
2. Be strong. Have courage.
3. It's better to be respected than to be liked.
4. I will always respect myself!

MAKE A CONNECTION

Brady and Jana talk about boys...and other things.

IN THE END...Brady has helped herself.

Brady learns to deal with peer pressure in a positive way. She learns to **stop the negative thinking when she feels pressured**, and she learns to change her own silly self-talk. She finds that most of the peer pressure has come from her mistaken ideas. Brady starts to change what she **says and does** with her group of friends. She chooses her own values, and she acts on her own values. She is **calm and strong**. She also **makes a good connection** with a special friend in the group.

Brady learns that friends will respect you on your own terms. They respect her confidence and her strength. Brady remains true to her friends and to herself. **Brady's problem is getting smaller.**

My Picture	What has happened? **OR** What might happen?
STOP. RELAX. What other self-talk could help me **avoid over-reacting** to the pressure to have sex?	**THINK SENSIBLY. BE CALM. BE STRONG.** What other **positive self-talk** could help me think sensibly' about this?
MAKE A PLAN	**MAKE A CONNECTION**

IN THE END...What is Likely to Happen?
Be honest. Be realistic.

Lesson Eight
Rudeness in Others

Ⓐ INTRODUCTION

The Social Story in Lesson Eight is about Tony. He is experiences a lot of anxiety when others say rude, unkind things to him. Why can't people always be fair?

Lesson Eight shows how "horriblizing" self-talk will almost always makes problems worse.

Ⓑ THE SCENARIO

1. Do a Guided/Shared Reading of Rudeness in Others: When Emotions Take Over.
   Create a Discussion about Tony's situation, his feelings, his reactions:
   • Re-read Tony's self-talk? What do you think about it?
   • What do you think about Tony's decision to quit playing soccer?

2. Now do a Guided/Shared Reading using the S.A.T. Plan.
   Create a Discussion about Tony's reaction this time:
   • Re-read Tony's sensible self-talk. What do you think about it?
   • How easy would it be for Tony to react calmly and strongly when someone says a rotten thing?
   • What do you think about Tony's decision to confide with his coach?

3. Have students complete the practice page on this topic, and share their ideas with 2 or 3 others.

Ⓒ FOLLOW-UP

Suggested prompts for Journal Writing:
• Imagine someone saying an unkind thing to you. Write 5 calm-strong self-statements to that.
• Create a cartoon entitled, "The Unkind Word" – and show an appropriate reaction to that.
• Pretend you are Tony's coach. As his coach, what advice would you give to Tony?

People are not always fair. Why?

SCENARIO

Sometimes the world is unkind. Tony is trying to make the soccer team at school and, at the try-outs, some of the other guys make jokes and rude comments about his soccer abilities. They don't seem to know that, sometimes, words can cut like a knife. Unkind words leave Tony feeling embarrassed and angry.

NEGATIVE THINKING

When Tony hears unkind words about his soccer playing, his brain is filled with **doubts and negative thoughts.**

"I **can't stand it** when they laugh at me. It proves I am no good."

"People who are unfair are **HORRIBLE!**"

"If they laugh at me, **I am the fool, I am the loser.**"

"People **should** be **fair and kind to me all the time.**"

EMOTIONS TAKE OVER

Tony's **exaggerated self-talk** leads to **exaggerated emotions**. If Tony repeatedly tells himself that unfairness is HORRIBLE, than it is – it is horrible only because he tells himself that it is. Since the other kids are making jokes about his soccer playing, Tony convinces himself that he is a **fool**, he is a **loser**. His negative self-talk brings him even more distress when he says to himself: "people **should** be fair and kind **all the time.**" These exaggerated ideas bring Tony a great deal of **anger and self-doubt**.

THE UNDER–REACTION

Tony thinks about dropping out of soccer. If he drops out, he will not have to put up with all of the unkind words and the jokes.

I should just quit soccer.

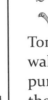

THE OVER-REACTION

Tony thinks that he might just walk up to the jokesters and punch them. That would stop them from joking around so much!

Come here you clowns!

IN THE END...Tony has not helped himself.

Dropping out of soccer is like an ostrich burying its head in the sand – by quitting soccer he will not really learn to deal with thoughtless words. Dropping out of soccer is only punishing himself; he enjoys soccer and he wants to make the team. Punching them will never stop the unkind remarks, and it will likely bring him more trouble – with the students, with the coach, and with his parents.

Dropping out of soccer is an **UNDER-REACTION**. The anger and embarrassment remain.
Punching those students is an **OVER-REACTION**. The anger and embarrassment remain.

Using the S.A.T. Plan – Rudeness in Others

I am going to change my self-talk whenever the world is being unfair. That might help me deal with this.

Tony makes the brave decision to examine his exaggerated thinking and to think of some ideas that will make his problem smaller. He knows that soccer is important to him. And, he would like to get along well with the guys on the soccer team. They should be his friends, not his enemies.

Tony creates a 4- part SAT (Sensible Acting & Thinking) Plan.

STOP. RELAX.

Tony thinks about how he is feeling when other people say unkind things. When he begins to feel anger or self-doubt he tells himself, "**Stop. Relax. Calm down for a while.**"

Tony practices those Stop-Relax statements until he becomes quite good at it. He refuses to let his **emotional brain** take control of his **thinking brain**.

At times Tony needs to walk away and give himself a few minutes to calm down.

THINK SENSIBLY. BE CALM. BE STRONG.

Tony does not allow his **exaggerated self-talk** to cause him distress. He knows that his feelings of self doubt and low anger come from these exaggerated thoughts.

THE TRUTH IS...

"I can't stand it when they laugh at me. I don't need to take their jokes **so seriously**."

"The world is not always fair and kind. I can **learn to accept** that."

"Just because someone jokes at my playing, it **does not mean** they are HORRIBLE."

MAKE A PLAN

I am going to be strong and calm – but not too soft or too angry.

MAKE A CONNECTION

Coach, can I talk to you for a few minutes?

IN THE END...Tony has helped himself.

Tony's SAT Plan helps him to deal with unfairness in a positive way. He learns to **stop the negative thinking when he hears unkind, unfair words**, and he learns to change his own exaggerated self-talk. He learns to put his thinking brain in control of the situation. He no longer tells himself how HORIRRLE-HORRIBLE-HORRIBLE it is when someone makes a thoughtless remark. He learns to lighten up when he hears a joke being made at his playing. Tony starts to change what he **says and does** at soccer tryouts. He is calm and strong. He also makes a good **connection** by talking to the coach about this.

Tony tries to remember that kids are sometimes thoughtless in their remarks; they are sometimes unfair – but that does not make them HORRIBLE. He stays calm and strong. **Tony is managing much better.**

Practice and Share – Rudeness in Others

My Picture	What has happened? **OR** What might happen?
STOP. RELAX. What other self-talk could help me **avoid over-reacting** to others' rudeness?	**THINK SENSIBLY. BE CALM. BE STRONG.** What other **positive self-talk** could help me think sensibly' about this?
MAKE A PLAN	**MAKE A CONNECTION**

IN THE END...What is Likely to Happen?
Be honest. Be realistic.

Lesson Nine
Parents Being Unfair

Ⓐ INTRODUCTION

The Social Story in Lesson Nine is about Felina. She is experiences a lot of frustration when others say insensitive things to her. Why can't people always be fair?

Lesson Nine shows how "horriblizing" self-talk makes rotten events even more rotten.

Ⓑ THE SCENARIO

1. Do a Guided/Shared Reading of Parents Being Unfair: When Emotions Take Over.
   Create a Discussion about Felina's situation, her feelings, her reactions:
   • Re-read Felina's self-talk? How is her self-talk likely to increase the frustration she experiences?
   • What do you think about Felina's decision to yell and scream at her father?

2. Now do a Guided/Shared Reading using the S.A.T. Plan.
   Create a Discussion about Felina's reaction this time:
   • Re-read Felina's calm-strong self-statements. What do you think about these?
   • How difficult is it to remain calm and strong when something rotten happens to you?
   • What do you think about Felina's plan (when someone next says something insensitive to her)?

3. Have students complete the practice page on this topic, and share their ideas with 2 or 3 others.

Ⓒ FOLLOW-UP

Suggested prompts for Journal Writing:
• Write a conversation between Felina and her dad (as she confides in him).
• Create a cartoon entitled, "The Insensitive Remark" – and show an appropriate reaction.
• Draw/color a poster that shows people how to react when an insensitive remark is made.

When Emotions Take Over – Parents Being Unfair

SCENARIO

Sometimes parents seem insensitive – especially with what they might say. It's true: Felina sometimes leaves her bedroom in a messy state, but her father's remarks cut deeply. When Dad sees her mess-filled room, he often says unkind things. His insensitive remarks leave Felina feeling hurt and embarrassed – and sometimes very angry.

NEGATIVE THINKING

Yes, Felina's room is often a mess, but when she hears those insensitive words from her father, her mind becomes flooded with **exaggerated, negative thinking**.

"I **hate-hate-hate** it when my father criticizes the way I keep my room. It makes me think that I am a complete slob."

"My father's remarks are unfair – and therefore he is **HORRIBLE-HORRIBLE-HORRIBLE!**"

"If he criticizes me, it means that **I am a slob and a total loser.**"

"Dad **should** be **fair and kind to me all the time.**"

EMOTIONS TAKE OVER

Felina's self-**talk** is **negative, unproven, and harmful**. It is her **negative thinking** that is causing **negative emotions**. Felina continually reminds herself that her father's remarks are HORRIBLE, and so it becomes just that – it becomes horrible. Further, Felina reaches the mistaken, unproven notion that she must be a **slob** and a **loser**. Her extreme sadness is compounded when she tells herself that her father **should** be fair and kind **all the time**. These rigid demands only add to Felina's **anger** and **insecurity**.

IN THE END...Felina has not helped herself.

Locking herself in her bedroom has done nothing to deal with the problem. Locking the door and pouting is like sweeping the problem under the rug. Throwing a tantrum and yelling at her dad is equally unwise; this will never stop the insensitive remarks, and it will likely cause more trouble in the family.

Locking the bedroom door is an **UNDER-REACTION.** The problem just gets bigger.
Throwing things around and yelling is an **OVER-REACTION.** The problem just gets bigger.

Using the S.A.T. Plan – Parents Being Unfair

Underreacting doesn't make it better. Overreacting doesn't make it better.

Felina thinks hard and then decides to challenge her own harmful, negative thinking and create a plan that will make her problem smaller. She wants to work out a plan that is win-win: she wins and her dad wins!

Felina uses the 4- part SAT (Sensible Acting & Thinking) Plan.

 STOP. RELAX.

Felina begins to examine how she is feeling when her father makes those insensitive remarks. When she begins to feel embarrassed or angry she tells herself, **"Stop. Relax. Don't take Dad's words so personally."**

Felina refuses to let her emotional brain take control of her thinking brain. She stays calm; she stays strong – and, she often sees the humor in her messy room.

 THINK SENSIBLY. BE CALM. BE STRONG.

More and more, Felina begins to check her own unproven, negative self-talk. She realizes that she upsets herself (more than her father does). Her anger and embarrassment come from her own unproven, negative thoughts.

THE TRUTH IS...

"Even if my room is messy, it **does not mean that I am a slob or a fool**. It means that my room is messy."

"I understand that my messy room bothers Dad; **it does not mean he is HORRIBLE**."

 **MAKE A PLAN**

When someone is not being sensitive to my feelings, I'm going to try to lighten up about that....I might even use a little humor.

 **MAKE A CONNECTION**

Felina has a talk with her dad. She tells him how she feels about his remarks. She also listens to how he feels. They make an agreement that is good for both of them. I win – you win!

IN THE END...Felina has helped herself.

Felina's SAT Plan helps her to relax – and to see some humor in her messiness. She learns to **stop the unproven, negative self-talk when she hears those insensitive remarks from her father**. She learns to change her negative, harmful self-talk. She learns to put her thinking brain in control of the situation. She no longer tells herself how HORIBBLE it is when Dad makes an insensitive remark about her bedroom. Best of all, she learns to see some humor in the situation. Felina starts to change what she **says and does** in those testy situations. She is **calm and strong – and sometimes funny**. She also makes a necessary **connection** around the whole bedroom issue – she works out a **win-win agreement** with her dad. Felina works out a **new plan** about her bedroom. Things are not always perfect, but they are a lot better. Most times, Felina doesn't under-react and she doesn't over-react. **Things are getting better.**

Practice and Share – Parents Being Unfair

My Picture	What has happened? **OR** What might happen?

STOP. RELAX.	**THINK SENSIBLY. BE CALM. BE STRONG.**
What other self-talk could help me **avoid over-reacting** to a parent telling me to clean my room?	What other **positive self-talk** could help me think sensibly' about this?

MAKE A PLAN	**MAKE A CONNECTION**

IN THE END...What is Likely to Happen?
Be honest. Be realistic.

Lesson Ten
Not Being Invited

Ⓐ INTRODUCTION

The Social Story in Lesson Ten is about Stan. His self-esteem is very low when he is not included, or not invited to parties or events. Why can't people always be fair?

Lesson Ten shows how low self-esteem is most often linked to negative, self-castigating self-talk.

Ⓑ THE SCENARIO

1. Do a Guided/Shared Reading of The Unfairness of Not Being Invited: When Emotions Take Over.
   Create a Discussion about Stan's situation, his feelings, his reactions:
   • How has Stan's Emotional Brain taken over his Thinking Brain?
   • Does not being invited to a party really prove that he is a loser? What does it prove?

2. Now do a Guided/Shared Reading using the S.A.T. Plan.
   Create a Discussion about Stan's reaction this time:
   • In what ways are Stan's new self-statements more positive?
   • How does Stan put his Thinking Brain in control?
   • Re-read Stan's 4-point plan? Do you think it is workable?

3. Have students complete the practice page on this topic, and share their ideas with 2 or 3 others.

Ⓒ FOLLOW-UP

Suggested prompts for Journal Writing:
• How can the Thinking Brain stay in control – even when rotten things happen?
• Create a cartoon entitled, "The Thinking Brain vs. the Emotional Brain."
• Draw/color a poster that invites people to a new movie: "The Thinking Brain vs. the Emotional Brain."

When Emotions Take Over – Not Being Invited

SCENARIO 10

On Thursday after school Stan overhears some of his friends talking. From the discussion he learns that one of their friends, Donny, is having a small party - and Stan has not been invited. Last month Stan had Donny come to his party, so what's up? Why is Donny leaving him out? How unfair! Stan is feeling **left out**, **unwanted**!

NEGATIVE THINKING

As Stan walks home from school, his blood begins to boil. That rotten Donny has cut him out of the party! His mind is flooded with negative self-talk:

"I have been left out of the group. That proves that I am a loser."

"I am now **second rate** to the group; **the guys don't really like me.** Maybe they think **I'm weird**."

"Donny **should** invite me to his party. He is being **totally unfair**."

"I **can't stand** this! This is a **catastrophe**!"

EMOTIONS TAKE OVER

Stan's **emotional mind** is racing – but it is racing in the wrong direction. Stan manages to convince himself that not being invited to the party is "**a catastrophe**." It is not unfortunate, to be left out of this party, it is a catastrophe! More than that, his emotional brain dictates, this must mean that he is "**second rate**," "**a weirdo**," and it must mean that the guys think he is "**a loser**." With all of these **unproven, exaggerated, negative ideas**, it is no wonder that Stan feels **depressed and unwanted**.

THE UNDER-REACTION

I'm never going to talk to that guy again! Or any of my friends!

THE OVER-REACTION

Hey Donny! I hear you flunked the test to be a human being!

IN THE END...Stan has not helped himself.

Never talking to Donny or his friends again has done nothing to help him feel better about this situation - this is only pretending to deal with the problem. And, it is likely that "embarrassing Donny in front of his friends" will not earn any respect from anybody - in fact, it will likely earn him a great deal of disrespect.

Not talking to his friends is an **UNDER-REACTION.** Stan's problem just gets bigger.

Embarrassing Donny is a vengeful **OVER-REACTION.** Stan's problem just gets bigger.

Using the S.A.T. Plan – Not Being Invited

> When my emotional brain tries to solve the problem, things almost always get worse.

Stan begins to change his mind about what he will do. He makes the decision to actively stop the negative self-talk of his **emotional brain**. He will make a plan that will make **his problem smaller**.

Stan uses the SAT-Plan to put his thinking brain in control.

 ## STOP. RELAX.

Stan starts to examine the negative self-talk coming from his **emotional brain**. When he begins to feel depressed or unwanted he tells himself, "**Stop. Relax. This isn't the end of the world.**"

Stan does not allow his **emotional brai**n to take over his **thinking brain**. He stays **calm and strong**.

 ## THINK SENSIBLY. BE CALM. BE STRONG.

Little by little Stan begins to trust his thinking brain. He does not allow his emotional brain to control his emotions with a lot of mistaken, harmful self-talk.

THE TRUTH IS...

"Not being invited to the party **does not mean the guys don't like me**. It **does not mean I am weird**."

"This is unfortunate. This is a bit of a **drag**. This is **not** a catastrophe. I **can** deal with this."

 ## MAKE A PLAN

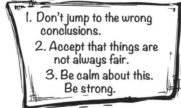
1. Don't jump to the wrong conclusions.
2. Accept that things are not always fair.
3. Be calm about this. Be strong.

 ## MAKE A CONNECTION

Stan has an honest talk about this with his good friend, Dana. It sometimes helps just to talk about things.

IN THE END...Stan has helped himself.

When Stan decides to trust his SAT Plan, he puts his **thinking brain** in control of his emotions. He learns to **stop the unproven, harmful self-talk when he is not invited to something**. He is careful not to reach the wrong conclusions. He begins to realize that being left out of a party is unfortunate, yes, - but it is **not a catastrophe**. It is a drag, yes, but it is not the end of the world. Stan realizes that it is best to accept some things as they are. He does not under-react to these disappointments nor does he over-react, he stays **calm and strong**. He also makes a helpful **connection** about this disappointment – by having a talk with one of his friends. Friends help.

Stan might be disappointed when these things happen – but he **refuses to get depressed**.

My Picture	What has happened? **OR** What might happen?

STOP. RELAX. What other self-talk could help me **avoid overreacting** to not being invited to a friend's party?	**THINK SENSIBLY. BE CALM. BE STRONG.** What other **positive self-talk** could help me think sensibly' about this?
MAKE A PLAN	**MAKE A CONNECTION**

IN THE END...What is Likely to Happen?
Be honest. Be realistic.

Lesson Eleven
Someone Not Liking You (Boyfriend/Girlfriend)

Ⓐ INTRODUCTION

The Social Story in Lesson Eleven is about Maham. She becomes greatly distressed when the strong feelings she has for someone else are not reciprocated. The world is sometimes unfair!

Lesson Eleven shows how the Emotional Brain can bring feelings of real inadequacy.

Ⓑ THE SCENARIO

1. Do a Guided/Shared Reading of Someone Not Liking You: When Emotions Take Over.
   Create a Discussion about Maham's situation, her feelings, her reactions:
   • How has Maham's negative self-talk influenced her emotions?
   • Maham thinks – magically – that the world "should" be fair. Is that a healthy attitude?

2. Now do a Guided/Shared Reading using the S.A.T. Plan.
   Create a Discussion about Maham's reaction this time:
   • In what ways are Maham's new self-statements more realistic?
   • How are these positive self-statements healthier?
   • Re-read Maham's 4-point plan? Do you think she will be successful? What if she is not?

3. Have students complete the practice page on this topic, and share their ideas with 2 or 3 others.

Ⓒ FOLLOW-UP

Suggested prompts for Journal Writing:
• What is a good way to get over a broken heart?
• Write lyrics to a song: "Getting Over You."
• "If I like someone, they should like me." Discuss that self-thought. Is that a healthy, reasonable attitude?

When Emotions Take Over – Someone Not Liking You

SCENARIO 11

Maham likes a guy in her class, Tristan. At school they talk and laugh a lot, and together they have a great time. But at the Friday dance in the gym, Tristan spends most of his time with another girl. Later, Tristan explains to Maham that he likes her – but only as "a friend." Maham is **heartbroken** and at night she **cries herself to sleep**.

NEGATIVE THINKING

Bedtime is the worst! Lying in the dark room Maham's mind is filled with **doom and gloom**:

"Why doesn't he like me – like I like him!"

"He probably thinks I am **ugly and stupid**!"

"He probably is **laughing at me** and telling his friends how **silly I am**. I bet everybody thinks I am a **loser**!"

"When I like someone a lot, that person **should** like me a lot! Life is **totally unfair**! Life is **rotten**!"

EMOTIONS TAKE OVER

On the pillow, the **emotional mind** of Maham is taking over. The sentences that come to her in the night are nothing but **doom and gloom**. Each night she manages to convince herself that she must be **silly and ugly** – and a **loser**. She **expects** the world to be fair; she **demands** that it is fair – since it is not, it must be **totally rotten**! The **doom and gloom self-talk** and the **unreasonable demands** are causing a lot of **heartbreak** for Maham.

THE UNDER–REACTION

At night, on her pillow, Maham has an idea: perhaps she will ignore Tristan altogether. She will no longer talk to him. They will no longer be friends!

THE OVER-REACTION

Maham has another idea. When Tristan is dancing with that other girl, she will walk up to him on the dance floor and make a scene. She will embarrass him. She will hurt him – like she is hurting.

IN THE END...Maham has not helped herself.

Ignoring Tristan altogether is a passive way to get back at Tristan. But this will never make her feel better; it will only cause her to lose a friend. On the other hand, making a scene on the dance floor will only make Maham look more desperate and out of control in front of her friends. This stunt will make things worse, not better.

Ignoring Tristan altogether is an **UNDER-REACTION** – and her problem just gets bigger.

Making a scene on the dance floor is a desperate **OVER-REACTION** – and her problem just gets bigger.

Using the S.A.T. Plan – Someone Not Liking You

I am noticing that my negative self-talk makes me feel rotten about myself....I am going to practice more positive self-talk.

Maham has second thoughts about what she will do. She makes the decision to stop the **doom and gloom** statements that come to her in the night. She will make a plan that **will make her problem smaller.**

Maham writes up a 4- part SAT (Sensible Acting & Thinking) Plan.

 ## STOP. RELAX.

Maham tries to put a stop to all the doom and gloom she has been feeling about Tristan. When she begins to feel down – especially at night, she tells herself: **"Stop. Relax. Things are not as bad as they seem."**

Maham tries to put her **thinking brain** in control. She tries to look at this situation in a reasonable, sensible, balanced way. She tries to be **calm and strong.**

 ## THINK SENSIBLY. BE CALM. BE STRONG.

Maham begins to understand that she is **upsetting herself** with **gloom and doom** statements – self-talk that is dangerous and wrong.

THE TRUTH IS...

"It would be nice to have Tristan like me as much as I like him, but he doesn't. This is **dis-appointing** – but it is **not a catastrophe**."

"This **does not mean** I am a **loser**." I am a **good person**. I can accept this. I **can** deal with this."

MAKE A PLAN

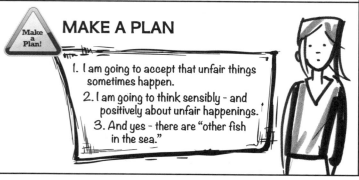

1. I am going to accept that unfair things sometimes happen.
2. I am going to think sensibly – and positively about unfair happenings.
3. And yes – there are "other fish in the sea."

MAKE A CONNECTION

Shari, I really like Tristan....What do you think I should do?

IN THE END...Maham has helped herself.

Maham refuses to get too upset about Tristan. She remembers that Tristan has a right to his own feelings. She decides to accept this and to try to value Tristan as a friend - this is the basis of her SAT Plan. She begins to see that **sensible self-talk** helps to prevent extreme sadness. She accepts that some things are unfortunate or disappointing – but they are never **catastrophes**. She knows, too, that **unfortunate things are manageable**. Maham does not under-react to these unfortunate things, nor does she over-react. Even in the darkness of her own room, she stays calm and strong. Maham makes an important connection by sharing her feelings with a friend she can trust.

Maham would like Tristan to like her a lot more – but her SAT Plan has helped her to see that this is only **disappointing** and to remember that she is a **good person** anyway. **Maham's is getting stronger**.

My Picture	What has happened? **OR** What might happen?
STOP. RELAX. What other self-talk could help me **avoid over-reacting** to someone not liking me?	**THINK SENSIBLY. BE CALM. BE STRONG.** What other **positive self-talk** could help me think sensibly' about this?
MAKE A PLAN	**MAKE A CONNECTION**

IN THE END...What is Likely to Happen?
Be honest. Be realistic.

Lesson Twelve
Cheating

Ⓐ INTRODUCTION

The Social Story in Lesson Twelve is about Cisco. He becomes extremely angry when he experiences someone cheating!

Lesson Twelve shows how extreme anger is directly related to extremely negative self-talk.

Ⓑ THE SCENARIO

1. Do a Guided/Shared Reading of Cheating: When Emotions Take Over.
   Create a Discussion about Cisco's situation, his feelings, his reactions:
   • Re-read Cisco's negative thinking. What are the strong words in this thinking?
   • Does Cisco's under-reaction solve the problem? Does his over-reaction solve the problem?

2. Now do a Guided/Shared Reading using the S.A.T. Plan.
   Create a Discussion about Cisco's reaction this time:
   • How has Cisco remained calm and strong – even when he has been cheated?
   • Cisco is taking a different attitude about cheating – how so?
   • How has Cisco tried to use humor to "lighten up" about the cheating?

3. Have students complete the practice page on this topic, and share their ideas with 2 or 3 others.

Ⓒ FOLLOW-UP

Suggested prompts for Journal Writing:
• Being cheated is not a happy thing – but it is also not the end of the world. Discuss this.
• Write a funny song: "You Cheat!"
• Write 5 sensible, positive (perhaps humorous) self-statements to use when you are cheated.

I can't stand it when people cheat!

SCENARIO 12

Cisco plays basketball after school. Some of the guys in the game are **not always fair and square**. These guys break the rules – so they are able to do better in the game. Cisco wonders why these people like to cheat; after all, it's only a game of basketball. Still Cisco is greatly troubled by this cheating and he often becomes **enraged**.

NEGATIVE THINKING

When someone breaks the rules in the basketball game, Cisco can feel the tenseness in his body. His heart beats faster, his face becomes flushed, he clenches his fists – and, his **negative self-talk** increases the anger he is feeling.

"Anyone who cheats in a game is **totally rotten**."

"I **can't stand it** when people cheat."

"I **need to get even** with cheaters."

"Cheating is **horrible, terrible, rotten**."

EMOTIONS TAKE OVER

Cisco's self-talk is filled with **horrible-izing** and **terrible-izing**. He manages to persuade himself that cheating is **not merely annoying**, it is **not merely disappointing** - it is **extremely terrible**. These extreme self-statements cause extreme emotions and, before long, Cisco's emotional brain is running the show. Cisco will not act **annoyed or disappointed**; he will act like an **enraged** person. In these games, Cisco **often loses control**.

THE UNDER–REACTION

That's it. I quit!

THE OVER-REACTION

You dirty cheats!

IN THE END...Cisco has not helped himself.

Giving up on basketball is only cheating himself. He loves basketball, and his friends are important to him. Punching someone would even be worse; violence only produces more violence; it is never a solution. When Cisco's emotional brain is in control, the solutions become lose-lose: he loses and his buddies lose.

Giving up on basketball is an **UNDER-REACTION.** Cisco's problem just gets bigger.

Punching someone is a violent **OVER-REACTION.** Cisco's problem just gets bigger.

Using the S.A.T. Plan – Cheating

Sometimes I think things are horrible, rotten, terrible. Maybe they are not....maybe I am exaggerating.

Cisco wonders what he should do about the cheating in the basketball games. In his quieter moments he realizes that everybody loses when he under-reacts or when he over-reacts. He makes the strong decision to look for a win-win outcome to this.

Cisco uses the 4- part SAT (Sensible Acting & Thinking) Plan.

STOP. RELAX.

Cisco pays attention to his emotions. When he notices his heart beating faster and his fists being clenched, he tells himself: **"Stop. Relax. Cool down. Don't get so serious about this."**

Cisco tries to think about the cheating a little differently. He tries to see some humor in this and to lighten up when these things happen. Cisco practices being **calm and strong**.

THINK SENSIBLY. BE CALM. BE STRONG.

Cisco is learning something important – if he tells himself that the cheating is merely silly or funny, he never becomes overly emotional.

THE TRUTH IS...

"Cheating is not **horrible** – in fact, it's just a **little silly**."

"Cheaters are not **terrible** – in fact, they are a little funny."

MAKE A PLAN

I am going to stop my horriblizing and terriblizing when unfair things happen.... I can react to unfairness by being strong and calm.

MAKE A CONNECTION

Cisco has a chat with his father about the cheaters. It helps to talk about things that are bothering him.

IN THE END...Cisco has helped himself.

Cisco learns to see cheating as a **silly, funny thing** – and **not** as a terrible, horrible, rotten thing. When he takes this view, he does not become enraged. When he takes this view, h**e does not under-react, nor does he over-react**. He **acts differently**. Often he brings some humor to the situation – and this wins some respect from his friends. As well, he makes a connection; he has a talk with his father about the cheating in the basketball games, and that talk has helped him feel better.

Cisco's SAT Plan has helped him to see that humor is sometimes a good way of dealing with troubling issues. When Cisco is able to lighten up on the inside, **he is able to lighten up on the outside**.

Practice and Share – Cheating

My Picture	What has happened? **OR** What might happen?

STOP. RELAX.	**THINK SENSIBLY. BE CALM. BE STRONG.**
What other self-talk could help me **avoid over-reacting** to someone who cheats?	What other **positive self-talk** could help me think sensibly' about this?

MAKE A PLAN	**MAKE A CONNECTION**

IN THE END...What is Likely to Happen?
Be honest. Be realistic.

Lesson Thirteen
Studying

Ⓐ INTRODUCTION

The Social Story in Lesson Thirteen is about Alexandra. She becomes overly frustrated when distractions around the house prevent her from studying for an upcoming test! Why can't people be fair!

Lesson Thirteen shows how negative self-talk allows the Emotional Brain to take control.

Ⓑ THE SCENARIO

1. Do a Guided/Shared Reading of Studying: When Emotions Take Over.
    Create a Discussion about Alexandra's situation, her feelings, her reactions:
    • Re-read Alexandra's negative thinking. How do these thoughts actually add to her frustration?
    • Does Alexandra's under-reaction solve the problem? Does her over-reaction solve the problem?

2. Now do a Guided/Shared Reading using the S.A.T. Plan.
    Create a Discussion about Alexandra's reaction this time:
    • Alexandra is trying to remain calm and strong – how difficult do you think this would be?
    • Examine Alexandra's sensible thinking – how are these more truthful (than the negative)?
    • Why might it be helpful to talk to her mother? Does this always work out for the best?

3. Have students complete the practice page on this topic, and share their ideas with 2 or 3 others.

Ⓒ FOLLOW-UP

Suggested prompts for Journal Writing:
• Draw a 2-pane cartoon of Alexandra – (1) thinking negatively, (2) thinking positively, sensibly.
• Write a short poem: "The Test" – including some of the key ideas from our lesson.
• "Not being able to study" – write about a personal experience on this.

> I NEED to study!
> Those two don't even care!
> I can't take it when people
> are unfair!

SCENARIO 13

Alexandra has an important math test coming up, but things are not running smoothly tonight. Her younger brother has the television on, her sister has her music playing – and both of them are not cooperating with her demands to keep quite! The math test is causing a lot of pressure for her – and brother and sister are causing a lot of frustration!

NEGATIVE THINKING

The math test is putting a lot of stress on Alexandra – and the noise from her brother and sister are making it worse! When the music is turned up, she can feel her own blood pressure go up.

"**I can't stand it** when those two won't cooperate."

"They are being **totally unfair** and I hate them for that!"

"This math test is **driving me crazy!**"

EMOTIONS TAKE OVER

Alexandra's self-talk is repeated (in her mind) over and over. She continues to focus on **how horribly unfair** her brother is acting and how horribly unfair her sister is acting. These thoughts are causing an **emotional overload** in her brain – and soon Alexandra will be in the panic mode. Her mind will be filled with **hate** and **anger** and **frustration**.

THE UNDER–REACTION

> Fine! I quit! I will fail the test and it will be YOUR FAULT!

THE OVER-REACTION

> I'll just pull the plug on the TV and laptop!

IN THE END...Alexandra has not helped herself.

Not studying – and failing the test is only punishing herself. That reaction will never make her brother and sister feel sorry; it will only make the feud become larger. Pulling those electrical cords may even be worse; this will likely cause a lot of yelling and screaming – and probably a fight! As Alexandra puts her emotional brain in charge, her reactions will only lead to more trouble. Emotional reactions almost always fail.

Not studying – and blaming brother/sister is an **UNDER-REACTION.** Her frustration just increases.

Pulling the electrical cords is a risky **OVER-REACTION.** Her frustration just increases.

Using the S.A.T. Plan – Studying

It seems I am either underreacting or over-reacting to things unfair. I am trying to be smarter....very calm and very strong.

Alexandra puts down her pencil, sits back in her chair – and she makes an important decision. She makes the decision to react to all of this frustration in a calm, strong manner. She knows that emotional reactions are almost always unsuccessful.

Alexandra sits down and creates a 4- part Sensible Acting & Thinking Plan.

STOP. RELAX.

Alexandra quietly thinks about her own emotions. When she notices her blood pressure begin to rise, she tells herself: **"Stop. Relax. Put the pencil down. Smile."**

Alexandra turns on her thinking brain – and she actively refuses to let panic and frustration take over. Alexandra works on being **calm and strong.**

THINK SENSIBLY. BE CALM. BE STRONG.

Alexandra works hard at being calm and strong. She helps herself do this by practicing **sensible, positive self-talk**.

THE TRUTH IS...

"People are not horrible just because they want to listen to their music or the television – sure, they are being a bit inconsiderate, **but I can manage that.**"

"**I will find a way** to study for this test. I **am able** to work out a **win-win plan** with my brother and sister. I can do that."

MAKE A PLAN

Excuse me guys....
Listen, I have a really important test coming up. I would really appreciate your turning the TV down while I am studying.

MAKE A CONNECTION

Alexandra talks to Mom about her study issues.

IN THE END...Alexandra has helped herself.

Alexandra learns to calm down **before** she reacts to the inconsiderate actions of her brother and sister. When she talks to them, her voice **is strong – but respectful**. She knows that this will **not always win their consideration** – but her chances are always better when she is able to show respect. And, she makes a good connection by discussing her study-time needs with Mom. She does not want to tell on her brother and sister, but to work out a study-time plan that would help all of them.

Alexandra's SAT Plan has allowed her **thinking brain** to deal with the problem. When she is able to **calm down** before she talks to her brother and sister, things have a better chance of working out.

Practice and Share – Studying

My Picture	What has happened? **OR** What might happen?
STOP. RELAX. What other self-talk could help me **avoid over-reacting** to a brother or sister distracting me?	**THINK SENSIBLY. BE CALM. BE STRONG.** What other **positive self-talk** could help me think sensibly' about this?
MAKE A PLAN	**MAKE A CONNECTION**

IN THE END...What is Likely to Happen?
Be honest. Be realistic.

Lesson Fourteen
Having Material Things

Ⓐ INTRODUCTION

The Social Story in Lesson Fourteen is about Chad. He becomes overly distressed when he thinks about all the money and material things some other kids have – and he does not! So unfair!

Lesson Fourteen shows that extreme sadness is most often related to destructive attitudes and values – and not from the money and material things you have or do not have.

Ⓑ THE SCENARIO

1. Do a Guided/Shared Reading of Having Material Things: When Emotions Take Over.
   Create a Discussion about Chad's situation, his feelings, his reactions:
   • Examine Chad's under-reaction: Why is this likely to make his problem even bigger?
   • Examine Chad's over-reaction: Why is this likely to make his problem even bigger?

2. Now do a Guided/Shared Reading using the S.A.T. Plan.
   Create a Discussion about Chad's reaction this time:
   • Re-read Chad's SAT Plan – how realistic is this?
   • Examine Chad's sensible thinking. Are these actually more reasonable and healthy?
   • Why might it be helpful to talk to his father?

3. Have students complete the practice page on this topic, and share their ideas with 2 or 3 others.

Ⓒ FOLLOW-UP

Suggested prompts for Journal Writing:
• Draw a 2-pane cartoon of Chad – (1) thinking negatively, (2) thinking positively, sensibly.
• How do advertisements (in magazines, on television, the radio, and the internet) form our attitudes about money and material things? Can we ever deny these attitudes and think for ourselves?
• List 5 inaccurate, exaggerated, dangerous attitudes linked to money and material things.

When Emotions Take Over – Having Material Things

SCENARIO 14

Many of Chad's friends have more that he does – more clothes, more electronic gizmos, more money to spend. And, when Chad pays a visit to his buddies, it is plain to see that their homes are nicer. It is true that Chad's friends are important to him – but not having as much as his friends often brings feelings of inferiority and insecurity.

NEGATIVE THINKING

When Chad is with his friends he cannot help but notice all of the things they have and his mind his flooded with self-doubts:

"They have everything and I have nothing; life is so unfair; **I can't stand it**!"

"The only reason they hang around with me is because **they feel sorry for me**."

"They must think I am a loser."

"**People with money are more important**."

EMOTIONS TAKE OVER

It is easy to understand why Chad might feel **so inferior, so insecure**. After all, television and magazine ads constantly remind us that our **feelings of self-worth are tied to products that we buy**. The idea that we need material things in order to feel worthwhile is an unproven, harmful belief. For sure, Chad's self-talk is focused too much on these **dangerous beliefs**.

THE UNDER-REACTION

I'm going to GIVE UP on those friends.

THE OVER-REACTION

You guys think you're so cool!

IN THE END...Chad has not helped himself.

By not hanging around his friends he is clearly losing out; his friends are important to him. Telling them off or fighting with them, will do the same thing – it will leave him without friends and feeling no better about himself. It is important for Chad to understand that both of these reactions are emotional reactions. Chad would do better to turn on his thinking brain.

Not hanging around his friends anymore is an **UNDER-REACTION** – and his insecurity only grows. Telling them off and fighting with them is an **OVER-REACTION** – and his insecurity only grows.

Using the S.A.T. Plan – Having Material Things

I'm going to use my emotional brain less....and my thinking brain more!

Chad wants to deal with his feelings of insecurity and inferiority in a **thoughtful way** – and not in an **emotional way**.

He decides to get rid of some stress – not to under-react and not to over-react. Chad works out a SAT Plan.

 STOP. RELAX.

Chad thinks about the times when he is feeling most insecure and inferior. He realizes that it is his **own negative self-talk** that is responsible for those bad feelings. He prepares himself for those moments, and when he begins to feel worthless or sad, he immediately tells himself: **"Stop. Relax. Don't upset yourself about this."**

Chad **actively refuses** to let his **emotional brain** deepen his feelings of inferiority. He learns to deal with these situations in a way that is **calm and strong**.

 THINK SENSIBLY. BE CALM. BE STRONG.

Chad makes up his mind not to be resentful of what his friends have. He will not envy what they have, nor will he be embarrassed for what he does not have. He learns to think **sensibly and positively about material things**.

THE TRUTH IS...

"People are **not more important** if they have expensive things."

"I may have less than some of my friends, but **that does not make me unlikable**."

"I don't need to be afraid or insecure when I am in a home that is nicer than mine. I am a strong person; I am a good friend."

 **MAKE A PLAN**

I'm going to think sensibly about material things. I'm not going to upset myself about things I can't control. I am a good friend, a good person – even if I have less than some others.

 **MAKE A CONNECTION**

Dad, does it ever bother you that we don't have as much as some other people?

IN THE END...CHAD has helped himself.

Slowly, steadily, Chad is becoming the master of his emotions. When he begins to feel insecure or inferior, he immediately stops his negative thinking. He reminds himself that clothes and electronic gizmos and skateboards and houses are only things. He is able to appreciate some of the things his friends are able to have – and, sometimes, to show this appreciation. **He learns to be strong and confident – and not to envy material things too much**. He makes a **connection** by having a money and materials chat with his own father. Chad's SAT Plan puts his thinking brain in control of his emotions. Importantly, he learns to change his own negative, defeating self-talk into positive, sensible self-talk.

My Picture	What has happened? **OR** What might happen?
![STOP Relax] **STOP. RELAX.** What other self-talk could help me **avoid over-reacting** to not having as much as my friends?	![Be Strong Be CALM] **THINK SENSIBLY. BE CALM. BE STRONG.** What other **positive self-talk** could help me think sensibly' about this?
![Make a Plan!] **MAKE A PLAN**	![Make a Connection] **MAKE A CONNECTION**

IN THE END...What is Likely to Happen?
Be honest. Be realistic.

Lesson Fifteen
Conflict with Friends (Girl)

Ⓐ INTRODUCTION

The Social Story in Lesson Fifteen is about Latoya. She finds that disagreements with her best friend may easily turn into arguments – and arguments may easily turn into personal, loud conflicts.

Lesson Fifteen shows that when disagreements become overly emotional, the conflict escalates; when disagreements are dealt with calmly and strongly, the conflict diminishes.

Ⓑ THE SCENARIO

1. Do a Guided/Shared Reading of Conflict with Friends (girl): When Emotions Take Over.
   Create a Discussion about Latoya's situation, her feelings, her reactions:
   • Examine Latoya's horriblizing self -talk: How does it lead to an under-reaction? An over-reaction?
   • Even if Latoya managed to get back at Marianne, what would be the long-term outcome of this?

2. Now do a Guided/Shared Reading using the S.A.T. Plan.
   Create a Discussion about Latoya's reaction this time:
   • What sensible self-talk helped Latoya to stay calm and strong?
   • Re-read the 4 parts to Latoya's plan. Are these reasonable and workable?
   • Why might it be helpful to talk to Latoya?

3. Have students complete the practice page on this topic, and share their ideas with 2 or 3 others.

Ⓒ FOLLOW-UP

Suggested prompts for Journal Writing:
• List 4 things that will almost always turn a disagreement into a major conflict.
• List 5 things that will almost always avoid a major conflict.
• Write a personal connection to resolving conflict. What do you try to do to solve conflicts?

Marianne lied to me. This is absolutely HORRIBLE!

SCENARIO 15

Latoya texts Marianne to ask her to go to the mall for some shopping. Marianne says she cannot go today because she has a lot of work to do. Later, Latoya sees Marianne at the mall – with three other girls. Latoya and Marianne are best friends – so why has she done this? Why has she been so dishonest? Latoya feels confused, hurt and angry.

NEGATIVE THINKING

At home, lying on the sofa, Latoya thinks about what her friend has done – and her mind is invaded by negative thoughts:

"She lied to me – that makes her **horrible**!"

"She lied to me – she **must not like me anymore**!"

"She lied to me - she must think I am a **loser**."

"**Our friendship cannot survive this**!"

EMOTIONS TAKE OVER

When Latoya first sees Marianne with the girls at the mall, she is surprised and disappointed. But as time goes on, she convinces herself that this act of disloyalty is **absolutely horrible**! Latoya's negative thoughts continue to produce negative emotions – and soon her mind is swimming with great **confusion, pain** and **anger**.

THE UNDER-REACTION

That's it! I am never talking to Marianne again! Never!

THE OVER-REACTION

I am going to get her back if it's the last thing I do! I HATE her!

IN THE END...Latoya has not helped herself.

Her idea to "never...speak to Marianne again" means that she will give up on her best friend. Her other idea – "I am going to get her back!" – is, likewise, something that will not help her in the end. "Getting back at people" never really makes them feel sorry, – it only makes them angrier. Back-and-forth revenge is always a lose-lose cycle. Latoya needs to understand that both of her ideas are emotional reactions. She needs to trust her thinking brain.

Giving up on their friendship is an **UNDER-REACTION** – and her hurt and anger grow.
Seeking revenge is an **OVER-REACTION** – and her hurt and anger grow.

Using the S.A.T. Plan – Conflict with Friends (Girl)

> Giving up doesn't make things better. Overreacting makes things even worse. I need to use my thinking brain.

Latoya decides that she will try to deal with her feelings of confusion, hurt and anger in a **logical way** (rather than an **emotional way**).

She decides to take control of her emotions and her actions – not to under-react and not to over-react. Latoya works out a SAT Plan.

STOP. RELAX.

Latoya thinks deeply about feelings of hurt and anger. She begins to examine her **own negative self-statements** that are producing those bad feelings. She then makes the brave decision to confront those thoughts. She says: **"Stop. Relax. This is not the end of the world."**

Little by little, Latoya is able to switch off the negative thinking and, thereby, switch off her **emotional brain**. She learns to think about what has happened in a logical way. She learns to be **calm and strong**.

THINK SENSIBLY. BE CALM. BE STRONG.

Latoya realizes that her own negative thoughts were making her feel worse and worse. Her negative thoughts were making her feel more hurt, more confused, more angry. Latoya thinks about what her friend has done.

THE TRUTH IS...

"This is not **horrible** – it is **disappointing**."

"This **does not mean** Marianne is horrible."

"This **does not mean** she hates me."

"This d**oes not mean** I am a loser."

"Our friendship does **not need to be over**."

"I **am strong**. I **can manage** this."

MAKE A PLAN

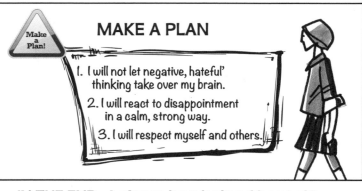

1. I will not let negative, hateful' thinking take over my brain.
2. I will react to disappointment in a calm, strong way.
3. I will respect myself and others.

MAKE A CONNECTION

Talking to Chad doesn't solve every problem – but it helps just to talk.

IN THE END...Latoya has helped herself.

Latoya is learning to switch off her negative self-statements. She is learning to switch off her emotional brain. She is able to tell herself, "Marianne has done something that **is not very nice**, and to see this as only **disappointing**." She knows that she can manage disappointment by **thinking logically and being honest** with Marianne. By talking to Chad, Latoya makes a connection and gains some emotional support.

As Latoya uses the SAT Plan she puts her **logical brain** in control of her emotions. She learns to switch off those dangerous self-statements and to turn on calm, sensible self-statements. **Latoya's SAT Plan is helping her to manage conflict in a strong, calm, logical way.**

My Picture	What has happened? **OR** What might happen?

STOP. RELAX.

What other self-talk could help me **avoid over-reacting** to a conflict with my friend?

THINK SENSIBLY. BE CALM. BE STRONG.

What other **positive self-talk** could help me think sensibly' about this?

MAKE A PLAN

MAKE A CONNECTION

IN THE END...What is Likely to Happen?
Be honest. Be realistic.

Lesson Sixteen
Conflict with Friends (Boy)

Ⓐ INTRODUCTION

The Social Story in Lesson Sixteen is about Lee. He becomes overly angry when his friends tease him.

Lesson Sixteen shows that the difference between a disagreement and a bitter argument is not so much what has happened – but the self-talk one has about that.

Ⓑ THE SCENARIO

1. Do a Guided/Shared Reading of Conflict with Friends (boy): When Emotions Take Over.
    Create a Discussion about Lee's situation, his feelings, his reactions:
    • Lee may decide to "ditch his friends for good." Why is this an emotional under-reaction?
    • Lee may decide to "let them have it." Why is this an emotional over-reaction?

2. Now do a Guided/Shared Reading using the S.A.T. Plan.
    Create a Discussion about Lee's reaction this time:
    • How does Lee put his Thinking Brain in control?
    • Re-read the 4 parts to Lee's plan. What is he going to remember when he feels upset with his friends?
    • Re-read Lee's sensible thinking. Which one do you like best?

3. Have students complete the practice page on this topic, and share their ideas with 2 or 3 others.

Ⓒ FOLLOW-UP

Suggested prompts for Journal Writing:
• Write a fictional story about Lee – as he stays cool and calm while working through disagreements with his friends.
• Do a mini poster that coaches people to solve disagreements in a peaceful, productive way.
• Draw a picture of Lee – showing his sensible thinking (about conflicts).

When Emotions Take Over – Conflict with Friends (Boy)

SCENARIO 16

Lee's friends want him to go camping on the weekend. Lee explains that he has to work, but they coax him to skip work and go camping instead. When he refuses to do this, they taunt him and say to him that friends are more important than work. Day after day the friends keep up the hassling. Lee is getting angry and impatient.

 ## NEGATIVE THINKING

Whenever Lee thinks about his friends remarks, the negative self-talk begins:

"Those guys are just trying to bug me – and **I can't stand that!**"

"These guys are becoming **totally rotten!**"

"My friends are **trying to make me feel like a loser** and I **hate-hate-hate** that!"

 ## EMOTIONS TAKE OVER

The more Lee thinks about his friends, the more upset he becomes. Over and over he reminds himself how **rotten** and **horrible** it is that they are acting this way. He sticks to the belief that his friends **should not** be that way. They **must** not be that way. The negative thoughts build on each other until Lee feels increasingly **angry** and **impatient** with his friends.

 ## THE UNDER–REACTION

One day Lee has an idea: "I should just ditch these guys. Get them out of my life."

I'm ditching those guys for good!

 ## THE OVER-REACTION

The next day Lee has another idea: "I should step up to those guys and let them have it!"

IN THE END...Lee has not helped himself.

His first idea to "ditch these guys" is an under-reaction that has only negative outcomes – he will lose important friends. His second idea to "let them have it" has, likewise, only negative outcomes – if Lee becomes overly aggressive or violent, he will likely lose his friends forever.

Ditching his good friends is an **UNDER-REACTION.** Lee's problem just gets bigger.
Letting them have it is an unnecessary **OVER-REACTION.** Lee's problem just gets bigger.

Using the S.A.T. Plan – Conflict with Friends (Boy)

I'm going to try to think about things differently. When my emotional brain takes over, things don't work out very well.

Lee decides to put his thinking brain in control. He wants to stand up for himself – but he does not want to needlessly lose his friendships.

He decides to not under-react and not to over-react. Lee works out a SAT Plan.

 STOP. RELAX.

Lee closely examines those things he has been telling himself. He accepts that his friends remarks are annoying but he begins to realize that his own **negative self-talk** is making it worse. When the negative thoughts begin, he now says to himself: **"Stop. Relax. What do these remarks really mean?"**

Lee is learning to avoid the negative self-talk that leads to great anger and impatience with his friends. He learns to think about what has happened in a more sensible way. He is learning to be calm and strong.

 THINK SENSIBLY. BE CALM. BE STRONG.

Lee is beginning to see how his own negative thinking is turning an annoying thing into a terrible, unbearable thing.

THE TRUTH IS...

"This is **not horrible** – it is **annoying**."

"This **does not mean** my friends are horrible."

"This **does not mean** they are trying to make me feel lousy."

"This is only an **annoying thing** my friends are doing – and I **can manage that**."

"I can deal with my friends remarks in a **strong and calm way**."

MAKE A PLAN

I'm going to remember that most things are only annoying or disappointing. They are NOT absolutely horrible. I am going to be smart, calm and strong.

MAKE A CONNECTION

When Lee starts to feel alone or left out, he connects with a friend – on the phone, by text message, on the computer – or in person. He is getting better at telling his friends how he honestly feels about things.

IN THE END...Lee has helped himself.

Lee is allowing his thinking brain to deal with his friends remarks. He is beginning to understand something very important – that his friends remarks are **only annoying**. He now reminds himself that his friends are being a little annoying today and he is able to respond to them with more patience and less anger. And, when he is feeling alone, he makes a point of **connecting** with a true friend.

When Lee decides to use the SAT Plan he is able to stick up for himself without over-reacting or under-reacting. He uses courage and honesty – rather than anger and aggression. **Lee's SAT Plan helps him to manage conflict in a sensible and strong way.**

Practice and Share – Conflict with Friends (Boy)

My Picture	What has happened? **OR** What might happen?
STOP. RELAX. What other self-talk could help me **avoid over-reacting** to a conflict with my friend?	**THINK SENSIBLY. BE CALM. BE STRONG.** What other **positive self-talk** could help me think sensibly' about this?
MAKE A PLAN	**MAKE A CONNECTION**

IN THE END...What is Likely to Happen?
Be honest. Be realistic.

Lesson Seventeen
Conflict with Teacher

Ⓐ INTRODUCTION

The Social Story in Lesson Seventeen is about Dina. She becomes extremely upset when she thinks her teacher is acting unfairly.

Lesson Seventeen shows that disputes are resolved much more effectively when one is able to remain calm and strong.

Ⓑ THE SCENARIO

1. Do a Guided/Shared Reading of Conflict with Teacher: When Emotions Take Over.
   Create a Discussion about Dina's situation, her feelings, her reactions:
   - How does Dina's under-reaction actually make her problem bigger (in the long run)?
   - How does Dina's over-reaction actually make her problem bigger (in the long run)?

2. Now do a Guided/Shared Reading using the S.A.T. Plan.
   Create a Discussion about Dina's reaction this time:
   - How does Dina effectively think more sensibly about Mr. Tindale's no-extension rule?
   - Part of Dina's plan is to remind herself that her teacher's actions may be "disappointing" – but are not absolutely "horrible, rotten, terrible." How does this help to reduce her personal stress?
   - Re-read Dina's sensible thinking. Do you think it is truly sensible?

3. Have students complete the practice page on this topic, and share their ideas with 2 or 3 others.

Ⓒ FOLLOW-UP

Suggested prompts for Journal Writing:
- Invent a character, a teacher – and write a story about "a teacher disagreement."
- Write a personal connection to Dina's story.
- Draw a line down the center of your journal page. In the left column write the self-talk that is likely to make a disagreement much worse; in the right column write the self-talk that is likely to make the disagreement much less.

SCENARIO 17

Dina's science project is due on Monday – and she wants to go out of town for the weekend. When Dina asks her teacher for a one-day extension on the project, he declines. Dina cannot understand why her teacher will not allow her an extra day on this project. What's the big deal! Whenever she thinks about it, she becomes extremely upset.

 ## NEGATIVE THINKING

On Friday evening, Dina is wondering what to do. She thinks about her teacher's no extension rule. Her mind is consumed with all sorts of negative beliefs about this:

"Mr. Tindale is **totally unreasonable**. **I hate him!**"

"Teachers have **no right** to boss me around. **I can't stand** this!"

"Mr. Tindale **should be fair** – or else he is a **rotten, rotten** teacher!"

 ## EMOTIONS TAKE OVER

Friday evening becomes worse for Dina. As she thinks about Mr. Tindale, the thoughts become more and more negative. Dina convinces herself that Mr. Tindale is totally unreasonable, extremely unfair – and, therefore, a horrible teacher. The negative thoughts continue to pile on one another all evening. At bedtime, Dina can hardly sleep. She is restless and extremely upset.

THE UNDER–REACTION

If Mr. Tindale is not going to cooperate, neither will I! I won't hand it in at all! So there!

 ## THE OVER-REACTION

Then, she has another thought: "I should act up in class. That will teach him!"

IN THE END...Dina has not helped herself.

Her first thought is to become very passive in Mr. Tindale's class – not to put her hand up or to smile or to acknowledge her teacher in any way. Will this really make her situation better? Her second idea is to become very aggressive – to act up and try to teach the teacher a lesson. Will this really make her situation better? Both of Dina's thoughts are likely to make her situation in school worse – not better.

Refusing to do her project is an **UNDER-REACTION.** The problem just gets bigger.

Acting up in class is a desperate **OVER-REACTION.** The problem just gets bigger.

Using the S.A.T. Plan – Conflict with Teacher

When things don't go as well as I hope, I often get very emotional, overly sad, overly angry. I think that I upset myself from the things I tell myself.

Lying in bed, Dina begins to question her own thoughts. She thinks about her two ideas – to refuse to do the project and to act up in class – and she begins to see that these will only make things worse for her in the long run.

Dina decides not to under-react and not to over-react. Dina makes a thinking plan - SAT Plan.

STOP. RELAX.

Dina starts to re-examine her own **negative beliefs** about what has happened. Yes, Mr. Tindale's no extension rule is disappointing – but is it really that bad? Dina decides to short circuit those negative beliefs inside her head. When the negative thoughts begin, she begins to tell herself: **"Stop. Relax. Cool down. Get over this."**

As time goes by, Dina learns to re-examine her own negative beliefs – and to manage them! She learns to think about what has happened in a **more reasonable** way, and to stay **calm and strong**.

THINK SENSIBLY. BE CALM. BE STRONG.

Dina refuses to let her own **negative beliefs** take control of her emotions. She begins to re-examine her negative thinking and stop the negative emotions.

THE TRUTH IS...

"Mr. Tindale's no extension rule is **disappointing** (rather than totally unreasonable)."

"I wish that Mr. Tindale would have allowed me an extension on the project, but he didn't. **This is not the end of the world**."

"This **does not prove** that Mr. Tindale is a rotten teacher, or a rotten person."

MAKE A PLAN

These things are NOT horrible, rotten, terrible....If I tell myself that they are only disappointing or annoying or a bit of a drag, I am able to act in a calm, strong way.

MAKE A CONNECTION

Dina has a long talk with her guidance counselor and talks with her grandma. She is always such a good listener.

IN THE END...Dina has helped herself.

Dina is becoming better and better at re-examining her own beliefs – especially when something unfortunate happens to her. She is beginning to recognize that **rotten feelings** come from **rotten beliefs** – more than they do from disappointing things that happen to us. By using the SAT Plan she is able to closely examine her own unproven, destructive beliefs, and change them to logical, helpful beliefs. Finally, she makes a **connection** with her guidance counselor – she realizes how important it is to talk to someone when things are not going well. And, she makes a good connection with her grandmother, someone she can always count on to listen and offer some advice. **Dina's SAT Plan is helping her to control her own emotions. She is learning to be calm and strong – even when rotten things happen.**

Practice and Share – Conflict with Teacher

My Picture	What has happened? **OR** What might happen?
STOP. RELAX. What other self-talk could help me **avoid over-reacting** to a teacher's rules?	**THINK SENSIBLY. BE CALM. BE STRONG.** What other **positive self-talk** could help me think sensibly' about this?
MAKE A PLAN	**MAKE A CONNECTION**

IN THE END...What is Likely to Happen?
Be honest. Be realistic.

Lesson Eighteen
Conflict with Sibling (Brother)

Ⓐ INTRODUCTION

The Social Story in Lesson Nineteen is about Juan. He often becomes infuriated when he thinks his brother, Dan, is being unreasonable.

Lesson Eighteen shows how a win-win (I win-you win) plan can lead to a peaceful resolution of a disagreement.

Ⓑ THE SCENARIO

1. Do a Guided/Shared Reading of Conflict with Sibling (brother): When Emotions Take Over.
   Create a Discussion about Juan's situation, his feelings, his reactions:
   • Re-read Juan's negative self-statements. Why are these statements largely untrue?
   • How do these negative self-statements actually "feed" an argument?

2. Now do a Guided/Shared Reading using the S.A.T. Plan.
   Create a Discussion about Juan's reaction this time:
   • How does Juan put his Thinking Brain in control?
   • Part of Juan's plan is to create a win-win plan to solve the dispute with his brother. How does this help to solve conflicts?
   • Juan has a talk with his older sister. Why is it important to talk to others about these things?

3. Have students complete the practice page on this topic, and share their ideas with 2 or 3 others.

Ⓒ FOLLOW-UP

Suggested prompts for Journal Writing:
• Create a "disagreement between brothers" scenario – and then write a win-win plan that could work to solve that disagreement.
• Write a personal connection to Juan's story.
• In your opinion, why do many disagreements escalate into fights? What is the answer?

Sometimes my brother is a real JERK!

SCENARIO 18

Juan's favorite show is on television – but his brother Dan is right now watching his show. Juan explains to Dan that this show is very important to him, and he asks his brother to give up the TV for a while. Dan is not cooperative, and he tells Juan to get lost. Juan is feeling infuriated.

NEGATIVE THINKING

Juan goes out into the kitchen. As he thinks about what has just happened, his brain is swimming with **negative self-talk**.

"Dan is being a **total jerk**."

"If I can't have what I want right now, **it is the end of the world**."

"**I can't stand this**."

"If Dan gets his way, **it means I am the fool**."

EMOTIONS TAKE OVER

As time goes on, the negative thoughts increase. When he goes out and sees his brother watching television, he can feel is heart pounding and the blood rush to his face. He reminds himself over and over that his brother is the worst jerk in the whole world.

As the negative thoughts build up in his brain, so do the negative emotions. He feels utterly infuriated.

THE UNDER-REACTION

I am not even going to look at Dan!

THE OVER-REACTION

A while later, Juan has another idea: "I am going to go in there and break the TV."

IN THE END...Juan has not helped himself.

Standing in the kitchen, his first notion is to never look at his brother again. But if Dan completely ignores his brother for a long time, he has entered into a lose-lose situation, and it is likely that his brother would become even less cooperative with him. Juan's next idea is to break the television. This, too, is lose-lose. A broken television will not make it any better.

Never looking at Dan again is an **UNDER-REACTION.** Juan's problem just gets bigger.

Breaking the television is a wild **OVER-REACTION.** Juan's problem just gets bigger.

Using the S.A.T. Plan – Conflict with Sibling (Brother)

If I can switch off my emotional brain and switch on my thinking brain things will turn out a lot better.

In the kitchen Juan is finally able to cool down and he considers his two plans of action. He realizes something very important – both of these ideas have I lose – you lose outcomes.

Juan then asks himself: Is there something I can do to create an "I win- you win" outcome?

**Juan thinks about a
Sensible Acting & Thinking Plan.**

STOP. RELAX.

Juan thinks about the **negative words** that are causing his heart to pound and his blood pressure to rise. Right away he decides to **switch off his emotional brain** and turn on his **thinking brain.** He tells himself: **"Stop. Relax. Don't over-react."**

Day by day, week by week, Juan learns how to stop the **negative words** – particularly when he thinks that someone might be acting in an uncooperative way. He learns to think about the uncooperative actions of others in different way. He stays **calm and strong**.

THINK SENSIBLY. BE CALM. BE STRONG.

Juan does not allow **negative words** to add fuel to **negative emotions.** He asks himself: What does this really mean? What is the big deal?

THE TRUTH IS...

"Dan might be **a bit uncooperative,** but this does not make him a **total jerk.**"

"If I can't have what I want right now, **it is the not end of the world**."

"**I can stand this.** I can be strong and calm."

"It is better to work out a **win-win situation** with Dan."

MAKE A PLAN

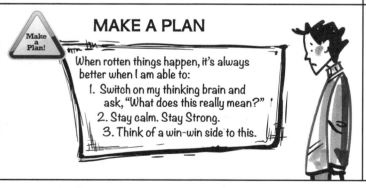

When rotten things happen, it's always better when I am able to:
1. Switch on my thinking brain and ask, "What does this really mean?"
2. Stay calm. Stay Strong.
3. Think of a win-win side to this.

MAKE A CONNECTION

Juan has a talk with his older sister. She is a good person to talk to about conflicts.

IN THE END....Juan has helped himself.

It is not always easy to turn off the emotional brain when someone is being uncooperative. But Dan is becoming more of an expert with his emotions. The trick, for Juan, is to think about what has happened and then to say to himself: **"What does this really mean?"** This question to himself helps Juan to stay calm, stay strong. In a calm-strong state of mind, he can act in his own best interest. His older sister is a good person for Juan to talk to – this is a helpful connection for him to make.

By using the SAT Plan he is able to suggest **win-win solutions** to other people. This does not always work perfectly – but it is much better than **highly emotional under-reactions or over-reactions.** **Juan's SAT Plan helps him to manage his own emotions – even when others are uncooperative.**

Practice and Share – Conflict with Sibling (Brother)

My Picture	What has happened? **OR** What might happen?

STOP. RELAX. What other self-talk could help me **avoid over-reacting** to a conflict with a brother?	**THINK SENSIBLY. BE CALM. BE STRONG.** What other **positive self-talk** could help me think sensibly' about this?

MAKE A PLAN	**MAKE A CONNECTION**

IN THE END...What is Likely to Happen?
Be honest. Be realistic.

Lesson Nineteen
Conflict with Sibling (Sister)

Ⓐ INTRODUCTION

The Social Story in Lesson Nineteen is about Tara. She tends to "blow her top" when she thinks her sister, Jenn, is being unreasonable.

Lesson Nineteen shows that constant bickering can be solved by creating to a calm, strong plan – and then by sticking to that plan.

Ⓑ THE SCENARIO

1. Do a Guided/Shared Reading of Conflict with Sibling (sister): When Emotions Take Over.
    Create a Discussion about Tara's situation, her feelings, her reactions:
    • Explain how Tara's "horriblizing" self-talk leads to an under-reaction?
    • Explain how Tara's "horriblizing" self-talk leads to an over-reaction?

2. Now do a Guided/Shared Reading using the S.A.T. Plan.
    Create a Discussion about Tara's reaction this time:
    • How does Tara put her Thinking Brain in control?
    • Tara's plan is to have a calm-strong discussion with her sister. Will this be easy?
    • Tara confides with her best friend, Mary Ellen. How will this help?

3. Have students complete the practice page on this topic, and share their ideas with 2 or 3 others.

Ⓒ FOLLOW-UP

Suggested prompts for Journal Writing:
• Create a "disagreement between sisters" scenario – and then write a win-win plan that could work to solve that disagreement.
• Write a personal connection to Tara's story.
• In your opinion, why does a lot of bickering never end? What is the answer?

When Emotions Take Over – Conflict with Sibling (Sister)

SCENARIO 19

Tara gets along with her sister, Jenn – but there are times when things get a little rough. Tara has asked Jenn not to wear her clothes, but when she comes home Saturday night, her bedroom door is open and her favorite jeans are missing. Tara knows that her sister has taken the jeans! Tara feels like blowing her top!

NEGATIVE THINKING

Tara sits on the bed and thinks about what Jenn has done – and one negative thought leads to another.

"My sister is being a **totally unfair.**"

"**I can't stand i**t when she takes my clothes."

"I need to **get back at her** for this."

"When people act this way, **it means they are horrible, terrible, rotten.**"

EMOTIONS TAKE OVER

As she sits on the bed, Tara's negative thoughts continue to build. Over and over she reminds herself how **horrible, terrible and rotten** her sister must be. She clenches her fists and grinds her teeth. **Why is her sister being so rotten**?

As the negative thoughts build up in her brain, so does the **anger**. Tara feels **like blowing her top**.

THE UNDER-REACTION

I'm going to lock her out and say nothing.

THE OVER-REACTION

This will teach her a lesson!

IN THE END...Tara has not helped herself.

Her first thought is to lock her room and say nothing to Jenn. It is true that her sister needs to get the message – but this action is likely to be confusing to Jenn, and she may wonder why Tara is acting this way. Tara's second idea, to throw Jenn's clothes around the house is also a confusing, hostile message. Yes, Tara needs to stick up for herself and communicate her feelings to Jenn – but if she does not communicate respectfully, it is likely that Jenn will become less cooperative as time goes on, and the sister-conflict will only deepen.

Saying nothing at all to Jenn is a confusing **UNDER-REACTION.** The stress only grows.

Throwing her clothes around the house is a needless **OVER-REACTION.** The stress only grows.

Using the S.A.T. Plan - Conflict with Sibling (Sister)

My angry plans are always my worst plans!

Tara decides to look at ways that will make her problem smaller. She wants to feel better about herself. She wants to deal with her feelings towards her sister in a more positive way. She wants to decrease her feelings of being angry at her sister and handle it in a calm way.

"I will work out a Sensible Acting & Thinking Plan," Tara tells herself.

 STOP. RELAX.

Tara begins to think about all of the negative emotions she has had about Jenn's actions. She reaches the conclusion that her own negative self-talk has made this situation much worse than it needs to be. When she thinks about what Jenn has done, she is able to tell herself: **"Stop. Relax. Don't make this such a big deal. Look for a solution, not a reaction."**

It is not always easy to stay cool, but Tara practices. She makes the decision to be a problem solver. Even when she thinks her sister is being unreasonable, she stays **calm and strong**.

 THINK SENSIBLY. BE CALM. BE STRONG.

Tara realizes that the first step in being a problem solver is to think sensibly about what has happened. She thinks about what Jenn has done:

THE TRUTH IS...

"Yes, my sister is being a **unfair,** but I can try to understand why she is doing this."

"**I can handle it** when she takes my clothes. I **can** be calm and strong about this."

"I **don't need to get back at her** for this. That only makes things worse."

"When people act this way, it **does not mean they are horrible, terrible, rotten** - just a little sneaky."

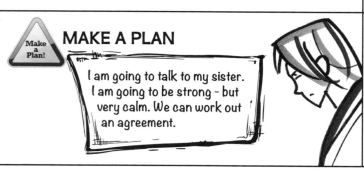 **MAKE A PLAN**

I am going to talk to my sister. I am going to be strong - but very calm. We can work out an agreement.

 **MAKE A CONNECTION**

Mary Ellen, do you ever have conflicts with your sister?

IN THE END...Tara has helped herself.

Tara makes the decision to be a problem solver rather than an under-reactor or an over-reactor. She realizes that, in dealing with her sister, it is very important to stay calm and strong. Tara needs to communicate her feelings to Jenn, and she needs to stick up for herself. And, she knows that if she can approach Jenn with calmness and respect she will be the problem solver she wants to be. The private chat with her best friend, Mary Ellen, is a good **connection** – she always listens and supports.

By using the SAT Plan Tara is refusing to react emotionally when things upset her. She is deciding to manage conflict in a smart, calm, respectful way. Yes, **Tara is learning to be a problem solver**.

Practice and Share – Conflict with Sibling (Sister)

My Picture	What has happened? **OR** What might happen?
STOP. RELAX. What other self-talk could help me **avoid over-reacting** to a conflict with my sister?	**THINK SENSIBLY. BE CALM. BE STRONG.** What other **positive self-talk** could help me think sensibly about this?
MAKE A PLAN	**MAKE A CONNECTION**

IN THE END...What is Likely to Happen?
Be honest. Be realistic.

Lesson Twenty
Conflict with Mother

Ⓐ INTRODUCTION

The Social Story in Lesson Twenty is about Ricky. When Ricky's mother demands that he come home and clean his room, he becomes extremely embarrassed and very angry.

Lesson Twenty shows that venting one's anger is a way of reducing one's inner stress – but, like all over-reactions, it usually makes problems bigger.

Ⓑ THE SCENARIO

1. Do a Guided/Shared Reading of Conflict with Mother: When Emotions Take Over.
   Create a Discussion about Ricky's situation, his feelings, his reactions:
   • How does Ricky make this rotten situation even more rotten?
   • Why is Ricky's plan to "not even deal with this" an under-reaction?

2. Now do a Guided/Shared Reading using the S.A.T. Plan.
   Create a Discussion about Ricky's reaction this time:
   • How is Ricky able to calm down and relax?
   • How has Ricky's SAT Plan made his problem smaller?
   • What are some other positive self-statements Ricky may have used?

3. Have students complete the practice page on this topic, and share their ideas with 2 or 3 others.

Ⓒ FOLLOW-UP

Suggested prompts for Journal Writing:
• Write a story about a character not getting along with her/his mom – be sure to show the character's self-talk that is related to that.
• List 5 tips for any young person who has a difficult relationship with her/his mother.
• Write about "getting along with mom."

When Emotions Take Over – Conflict with Mother

SCENARIO 20

Ricky thinks that his own room is his own business. Yet, his mom reminds him to clean up and to make his bed. On Friday, Ricky is at his friend's house and his mom calls him on his cell. She demands that he come home and clean his messy room. Ricky can't believe it – why would his mom do this? Ricky feels embarrassed and angry.

 NEGATIVE THINKING

When Ricky hangs up the phone, his mind is racing with **negative thoughts** about what has happened.

"This makes me **look like** an idiot in front of my friend."

"My friend will think I am a **total loser.**"

"Mom is being totally unreasonable and I **hate-hate-hate** her for this.

"This is a **totally rotten** day for me."

 EMOTIONS TAKE OVER

Standing beside the phone, Ricky continues to think about his mom's call. And he continues to convince himself how totally rotten this must be, and how **totally unreasonable** his mom must be, and what a total loser he must be.

His mind is filled with negative thinking and his body is filled with negative emotions. Ricky feels **extremely embarrassed and extremely angry.**

 **THE UNDER-REACTION**

I WON'T clean my room – but I will SAY THAT I DID!

  **THE OVER-REACTION**

Why are you being so rotten to me!

IN THE END...Ricky has not helped himself.

He thinks that he should pretend that he cleaned his room. This is an understandable reaction – but it does little to solve anything. Billy is only sweeping his problems under the carpet. His other idea is to go home and yell at his mother. This too is understandable: anger is a way of dealing with stress – but it does not solve the problem with his mother. This too is like sweeping his problems under the carpet.

Going home and refusing to clean his room is an angry **UNDER-REACTION.** Things just get worse. Yelling at his mother is a reckless, irresponsible **OVER-REACTION.** Things just get worse.

Using the S.A.T. Plan – Conflict with Mother

Sometimes my self-talk is silly, unproven, destructive.

As Ricky walks home from his friend's house, he is able to calm down and think about what has happened. He thinks about his idea to not do what his mom said. Will that solve anything? He thinks about his idea to yell at his mother. Will that solve anything?

Ricky changes his mind. He will deal with the problem reasonably – not emotionally. Ricky decides to follow the 4-step SAT Plan.

 ## STOP. RELAX.

As Ricky walks home, he realizes that he cannot solve the problem reasonably if he is full of anger. And, he recognizes that his anger increases whenever he thinks about **how rotten and terrible** his mom has acted.

Ricky tells himself: "**Stop. Relax. Be calm. Be strong.**

As the days go by, Ricky learns to **calm down and relax** before he talks to his mom about a problem. Sometimes he needs time to do this. If he waits for a few minutes and takes some time to **calm down'** and to **think sensibly'** about what has happened, he is able to be a **better problem solver.**

 ## THINK SENSIBLY. BE CALM. BE STRONG.

Ricky is beginning to see that his anger and embarrassment relate more to his negative, unproven, silly self-talk.

THE TRUTH IS...

"There is **no reason to believe** that my friend will think I am a loser. This is **unproven, silly thinking.**"

"If I think Mom is being unreasonable, **I can try to understand that**, and I certainly **don't have to hate her** for being that way."

"This is **not fun**, but **it isn't really the end of the world**. I **can manage** a little disappointment."

MAKE A PLAN

I'm going to remember that most things are NOT horrible' – they are only unfortunate.' I'm going to be a problem solver' – not a complainer.

MAKE A CONNECTION

Yeah, I know, Ricky. Sometimes my parents bug me, too. I think we all experience that sometimes.

IN THE END...Ricky has helped himself.

Ricky makes the brave decision to act' on the conflict with his mother. But, he will not under-react' nor will he over-react.' Ricky realizes he has never dealt with conflict very well when he was angry – and so, the first step in being a good conflict manager' is to **cool down and relax before talking to anyone.** He sees, too, that if he is able to connect with a good friend, he feels much better – good friends listen and don't make judgments.'

When Ricky uses the SAT Plan he has a better chance of getting things he really wants. Things don't always work out perfectly, but they work out much better. It is better to **stay calm, stay strong.**

Practice and Share – Conflict with Mother

My Picture	What has happened? **OR** What might happen?
STOP. RELAX. What other self-talk could help me **avoid over-reacting** to my mother?	**THINK SENSIBLY. BE CALM. BE STRONG.** What other **positive self-talk** could help me think sensibly about this?
MAKE A PLAN	**MAKE A CONNECTION**

IN THE END...What is Likely to Happen?
Be honest. Be realistic.

Lesson Twenty-one
Conflict with Father

Ⓐ INTRODUCTION

The Social Story in Lesson Twenty-one is about Rosalina. When Rosalina's father declines her request for a weekly allowance, she becomes very sad, and very angry.

Lesson Twenty-one shows that when emotions take over in conflict situations, problems often get bigger.

Ⓑ THE SCENARIO

1. Do a Guided/Shared Reading of Conflict with Father: When Emotions Take Over.
   Create a Discussion about Rosalina's situation, her feelings, her reactions:
   • Examine Rosalina's negative conclusions about her father. Are these necessarily true?
   • Rosalina's father refused to give her an allowance. Does this make him a rotten father?

2. Now do a Guided/Shared Reading using the S.A.T. Plan.
   Create a Discussion about Rosalina's reaction this time:
   • How is Rosalina able to calm down and relax?
   • Re-read the section on "the Truth is." How are these conclusions about her father smarter (than her previous negative conclusions)?
   • What do you think caused Rosalina to form such dire, exaggerated conclusions about her father?

3. Have students complete the practice page on this topic, and share their ideas with 2 or 3 others.

Ⓒ FOLLOW-UP

Suggested prompts for Journal Writing:
• Write a story about a character not getting along with her/his dad – be sure to show the character's self-talk that is related to that.
• List 5 tips for any young person who has a difficult relationship with her/his dad.
• Write a short piece about "getting along with Dad."

When Emotions Take Over – Conflict with Father

SCENARIO 21

Rosalina thinks that she does not have enough money, so she talks to her dad about increasing her weekly allowance.' Rosalina's dad says that he cannot afford to give her more money every week – and that she should try to get an after-school job. Rosalina thinks that her dad is just being stubborn and unfair. She is feeling **very sad, very angry.**

NEGATIVE THINKING

After their discussion, Rosalina thinks about what her father said.

"Dad could afford to give me some money if he really wanted to. He just doesn't want to help me out. He is being selfish. He **doesn't even care** about his only daughter."

"This proves that Dad is being a r**otten father**."

EMOTIONS TAKE OVER

Rosalina has only negative thoughts about her father's decision. She convinces herself that her father is unreasonable, unfair and selfish. She thinks that her father must' be fair all the time, and that he must' agree with the allowance – and, if not, it proves that he is a **rotten father.'** These are **extreme, rigid beliefs,** and it is no wonder that Rosalina is feeling **great sadness, great anger.**

THE UNDER–REACTION

THE OVER-REACTION

IN THE END...Rosaline has not helped herself.

She might think that totally ignoring Dad' will make him sorry, or make him change his mind about the allowance, but that is not likely to happen. She might think that stealing the money she wants' will also make him sorry or make him change his mind about the allowance, but that too is not likely to happen. Both of these actions are likely to make things worse. In the end, she will have made her problems worse, not better.

Ignoring her father' is a flimsy, attention-seeking **UNDER-REACTION.** The problem is still there.
Stealing money' is a dangerous, attention-seeking **OVER-REACTION.** The problem is still there.

Using the S.A.T. Plan – Conflict with Father

"'Ignoring dad' is an under-reaction. 'Stealing money' is an over-reaction. I need a sensible reaction."

After a while, Rosalina thinks about her plans to ignore her father or to steal the money she needs. Then she asks herself: Will these plans really solve the problem? Will they really make anybody sorry? Will they make my situation better?

Rosalina's answers to herself are: "No, no, and no. It is better to work out a SAT Plan."

STOP. RELAX.

Rosalina thinks about her own **negative self-talk,** and she recognizes that **she may be upsetting herself.** Rosalina wants to put her thinking brain in control of this, and she tells herself: **"Stop. Relax. Is it really that bad?"**

Rosalina comes to realize that the **first step of the SAT Plan** is the most important. By telling herself to stop and relax, she is telling her emotional brain to **step out** and her thinking brain to **step in.**

THINK SENSIBLY. BE CALM. BE STRONG.

Rosalina is becoming more aware of the power of self-talk. She knows that if she tells herself something is horrible and rotten, then it is. On the other hand, if she sees that same thing as only disappointing, then it is that.

THE TRUTH IS...

"Dad's decision about the allowance **does not prove** that he is totally unfair – and it **does not prove** that he is a rotten father."

"This is **only disappointing.** I can deal with that."

MAKE A PLAN

1. I'm going to think sensibly about what has happened.
2. I'm going to be very calm, very strong.
3. I'm going to work out a solution with Dad.

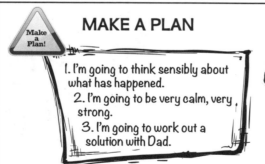

MAKE A CONNECTION

Mom, I'm feeling frustrated. Can I talk to you about something?

IN THE END...Rosaline has helped herself.

As Rosalina thinks about her decisions to ignore her father or to steal money, she realizes that these are ways for her to get attention. Her thinking brain tells her that seeking negative attention does not make life any better for her – and, probably, these attention-seeking actions would only make things worse. When she has troubles like this, she **connects** with Mom – she listens and helps out with some advice.

A **Sensible Acting and Thinking Plan** helps to put Rosalina in charge of her own emotions. It is a way of responding to disappointment that is **strong** and **calm** and **smart.**

Practice and Share – Conflict with Father

My Picture	What has happened? **OR** What might happen?

STOP. RELAX. What other self-talk could help me **avoid over-reacting** to my father?	THINK SENSIBLY. BE CALM. BE STRONG. What other **positive self-talk** could help me think sensibly' about this?

MAKE A PLAN	MAKE A CONNECTION

IN THE END...What is Likely to Happen?
Be honest. Be realistic.

Lesson Twenty-two
Failing a Test

Ⓐ INTRODUCTION

The Social Story in Lesson Twenty-two is about Galen. When Galen failed his math test, he became very depressed, very worried.

Lesson Twenty-two shows that negative thinking about an unfortunate happening often leads to feelings of distress and low self-esteem.

Ⓑ THE SCENARIO

1. Do a Guided/Shared Reading of Failing a Test – When Emotions Take Over.
   Create a Discussion about Galen's situation, his feelings, his reactions:
   • Does failing a math test prove that Galen is stupid? What does it prove or demonstrate?
   • Does failing a math test mean that Galen's life is ruined? What does it prove or demonstrate?

2. Now do a Guided/Shared Reading using the S.A.T. Plan.
   Create a Discussion about Galen's reaction this time:
   • Re-read Galen's sensible thinking. How are these thoughts more correct, more positive?
   • Re-read Galen's plan. How realistic is his plan? Do you think he can follow through with it?
   • What do you think Galen's mom may advise him to do?

3. Have students complete the practice page on this topic, and share their ideas with 2 or 3 others.

Ⓒ FOLLOW-UP

Suggested prompts for Journal Writing:
• Assume that Galen has written to the newspaper, asking for some advice about the difficulty he has with math. As the advice columnist, write back to him.
• Draw Galen – and include his positive, sensible self-talk (about his difficulties with math).
• Make a connection to Galen's situation. Have you ever been greatly worried about not doing well at a school subject (or possibly something else)?

When Emotions Take Over – Failing a Test

SCENARIO 22

Galen sits in his desk, waiting for the results of his math test. Finally the teacher drops the paper onto the desk and he quickly turns it over. It is not good. Galen has failed an important test. Now, he wonders what his parents will say.

Galen is feeling depressed and very worried.

 ## NEGATIVE THINKING

Galen decides to walk home from school alone. His mind is filled with troubled thoughts:

"This **proves I am stupid**."

"**My life is ruined**."

"My parents **will kill me!**"

"Failing a math test is **horrible, rotten, terrible**."

 ## EMOTIONS TAKE OVER

All the way home, the negative thoughts keep coming and growing. Galen continues to tell himself that failing the math test **proves he is stupid and worthless**. He continues to tell himself how rotten this must be. He continues to tell himself how **frightfully upset his parents will be**.

By the time Galen arrives home, he is **extremely depressed and totally worried** about failing.

THE UNDER-REACTION

I'm keeping this a secret!

THE OVER-REACTION

Mr. Dale is a no-good teacher. This is all his fault!

IN THE END...Galen has not helped himself.

Not telling his parents' is avoiding the truth – and this will continue to bother him. Whining and complaining and blaming the teacher' is, also, **avoiding the truth**. Neither of these ideas will help Galen deal with failure. Sometimes people want to hide the truth – but it always comes back to bite them. Galen has not had the right idea to deal with failing that math test.'

Not telling his parents' is a weak **UNDER-REACTION.** The depression and worry will still be there.
Blaming the teacher' is an unfair **OVER-REACTION.** The depression and worry will still be there.

Using the S.A.T. Plan – Failing a Test

This is not the easy way out...but I am going to face up to this!

Galen remembers something that his father once told him: "It is better to face things straight on – then they don't become so scary." With that memory, he makes the decision to deal with his failure straight on.

That night, Galen summons his courage and works out a Sensible Acting and Thinking Plan.

STOP. RELAX.

Galen takes charge of his emotions. Whenever he begins to feel depressed or frightened, he tells himself: **"Stop. Relax. Is failing a math test really that bad?"**

Galen does not want his emotions to get the best of him. By telling himself to stop and relax, he is able to move forward bravely and smartly.

THINK SENSIBLY. BE CALM. BE STRONG.

Galen starts to examine all of the things that he had been telling himself (about failing the math test). He realizes that most of his self-talk amounts to **unproven, exaggerated thinking.**
THE TRUTH IS...

"Failing a math test **does not prove I am stupid** – it only proves I failed a math test.
"**My life is not ruined.** That is silly."
"My **parents might be unhappy for a while, but they certainly will not kill me!**"
"Failing a math test **is not** horrible, rotten, terrible – it is disappointing."
"It is normal to be c**oncerned** about failing a math test; it is **not healthy** to be frightened and depressed."

MAKE A PLAN

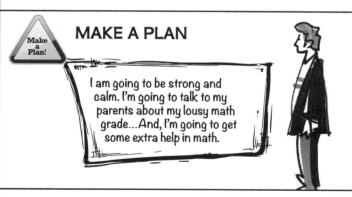

I am going to be strong and calm. I'm going to talk to my parents about my lousy math grade...And, I'm going to get some extra help in math.

MAKE A CONNECTION

Mom, I'm really concerned about math... It's really difficult for me. What do you think I should do?

IN THE END...Galen has helped himself.

It was not easy for Galen to face his own fears – but he did. He realized that most of those fears came from his own unproven, exaggerated self-talk. Failing the math test was horrible – **only if he told himself** it was horrible. Galen reminded himself that failing a math test was not the end of the world' – it was only disappointing. He knew his parents would be upset, but they would get over it – and so would he! He made an important connection when he sat down with his mom and talked honestly about how he felt. **Galen's Sensible Thinking and Sensible Acting is helping him to deal with failing in a healthy way.**

Practice and Share – Failing a Test

My Picture	What has happened? **OR** What might happen?

STOP. RELAX.

What other self-talk could help me **avoid over-reacting** to a failing grade in math?

THINK SENSIBLY. BE CALM. BE STRONG.

What other **positive self-talk** could help me think sensibly' about this?

MAKE A PLAN

MAKE A CONNECTION

IN THE END...What is Likely to Happen?
Be honest. Be realistic.

Lesson Twenty-three

Failing a Job Interview

Ⓐ INTRODUCTION

The Social Story in Lesson Twenty-three is about Sienna. When Sienna failed to get the job for which she applied, she became very sad and insecure.

Lesson Twenty-three shows that extreme sadness and insecurity are strongly tied to "what I believe to be true" about an unfortunate happening.

Ⓑ THE SCENARIO

1. Do a Guided/Shared Reading of Failing a Job Interview: When Emotions Take Over.
   Create a Discussion about Sienna's situation, her feelings, her reactions:
   • Does failing to get a job prove that Sienna is no good? What does it prove or demonstrate?
   • Does failing to get one job mean that Sienna will never get a job? What does it prove?

2. Now do a Guided/Shared Reading using the S.A.T. Plan.
   Create a Discussion about Sienna's reaction this time:
   • What do you think about Sienna's plan to keep trying, trying, trying? Is that not risky?
   • Sienna decided to ask her mom for some tips on getting a job. Who else might she ask?
   • What would you do if you were Sienna?

3. Have students complete the practice page on this topic, and share their ideas with 2 or 3 others.

Ⓒ FOLLOW-UP

Suggested prompts for Journal Writing:
• Write a short scene: your character is coming home from a job he/she failed to get; be sure to show the character's self-talk – will it be positive or negative?
• Make a list of 5 healthy attitudes about applying for any job.
• Can you make a connection to this theme? Have you ever applied for a job?

When Emotions Take Over – Failing a Job Interview

No one will ever hire me. I just know it!

SCENARIO 23

Sienna is excited. Did she get that job she applied for? She opens her email – but, no, she did not get the job. Sienna worked hard to prepare for the interview, but the job was given to someone else. She thinks that she has failed.

Sienna is feeling extremely sad and insecure.

NEGATIVE THINKING

As she sits there, in front of her computer, Sienna thinks about the email. She thinks about the job interview. She thinks about her failure.

"I **will never** get a job."

"Who would ever h**ire me**, anyway?"

"This proves **I am no good**."

"Now everyone will know h**ow stupid I am**."

"This is totally **horrible, terrible, rotten**."

EMOTIONS TAKE OVER

All evening, the negative thoughts continue. Sienna is able to convince herself, over and over, that failing a job interview means that she is a failure as a person. Her unproven, exaggerated thoughts cause her to feel stupid and worthless.

By bedtime, Sienna feels **very sad and very insecure**.

THE UNDER-REACTION

No, I have not talked to anyone about a job.

THE OVER-REACTION

Dear Rotten Person...

IN THE END...Sienna has not helped herself.

If Sienna tries to hide the truth she will likely worry that someone will one day find out. This idea is not really helping her feel better about herself – not in the long run. If Sienna sends that person a hate-letter she is only trying to make herself feel better – but this will not help her, not in the long run.

Not telling anyone about the interview is an **UNDER-REACTION**. Problems stay the same.
Sending a hate-letter is an irresponsible **OVER-REACTION**. Problems stay the same.

Using the S.A.T. Plan – Failing a Job Interview

I am not going to hide my head like an ostrich!

Sienna thinks about her choices. She does not want to act like an ostrich' – a bird that hides its head in the sand' when it is afraid of something. She knows in her heart that problems need to be faced head-on – and with courage.'

Sienna decides to act courageously. She writes up a Sensible Acting & Thinking Plan.

STOP. RELAX.

Sienna knows that she is upsetting herself about her failure to get the job. She needs turn off her emotional brain and turn on her thinking brain. Whenever she thinks about her failure to get the job, she tells herself: **"Stop. Relax. Don't get too upset about this."**

Sienna tries hard to think sensibly about failing at things. She examines her **negative self-talk** and she works hard to stop it.'

THINK SENSIBLY. BE CALM. BE STRONG.

Sienna examines her own unproven, **exaggerated thinking.**

THE TRUTH IS...

"I **will** get a job. I just need to keep trying."

"There are probably lots of people who would **hire me**. I need to have **confidence in** myself."

"This **does not prove** I am no good. It proves that I did not get the job this time. That's all."

"People will not think I am **stupid just because I did not get the job I wanted. That is silly thinking.**"

"This is **disappointing**. It is **not the end of the world.**"

MAKE A PLAN

1. I am going to keep on trying, trying, trying.
2. I am going to think courageously.
3. If I don't get a job, I will be proud of my courage.

MAKE A CONNECTION

Mom, I've got another job interview tomorrow...Any tips?

IN THE END...Sienna has helped herself.

Sienna refuses to be an ostrich. She makes the brave decision to look closely at what she is telling herself about failure. Sienna realizes that failure is made worse when she makes up harmful, unproven self-talk. The truth is: **negative thinking is causing her to feel much worse than she needs to.** She comes to accept that we all fail' at things sometimes – and that is okay. She is learning to pat herself on the back for being brave, taking risks, and trying out for things. And, whenever she tries out for things she has a talk with Mom. Sienna's SAT Plan **is working** – she might still fail at things, but she does not become overly sad' or overly insecure' about these things. **She is learning to be disappointed' – that's all!**

Practice and Share – Failing a Job Interview

My Picture	What has happened? **OR** What might happen?

STOP. RELAX. What other self-talk could help me **avoid over-reacting** to not getting the job I want?	**THINK SENSIBLY. BE CALM. BE STRONG.** What other **positive self-talk** could help me think sensibly' about this?

MAKE A PLAN	**MAKE A CONNECTION**

IN THE END...What is Likely to Happen?
Be honest. Be realistic.

Lesson Twenty-four
Getting Fired from the Job

ⓐ INTRODUCTION

The Social Story in Lesson Twenty-four is about Rory. When Rory was fired from his job, he reached the conclusion that he was a loser and became depressed.

Lesson Twenty-four shows that feelings of depression are strongly tied to illogical conclusions about the "rotten thing" that has happened.

ⓑ THE SCENARIO

1. Do a Guided/Shared Reading of Getting Fired: When Emotions Take Over.
    Create a Discussion about Rory's situation, his feelings, his reactions:
    • Does getting fired from a job prove that Rory is a loser? What does it prove or demonstrate?
    • Is getting fired from a job absolutely horrible, rotten, terrible? If not, what is it?

2. Now do a Guided/Shared Reading using the S.A.T. Plan.
    Create a Discussion about Rory's reaction this time:
    • Rory has made the decision to "have a brave voice." What does that mean?
    • Rory has made the decision to "never get down" on himself if things don't work out. What does that mean?
    • What advice would you give to Rory?

3. Have students complete the practice page on this topic, and share their ideas with 2 or 3 others.

ⓒ FOLLOW-UP

Suggested prompts for Journal Writing:
Write a short scene: your character has just been fired from his/her job. How can he/she avoid over-reacting to this rotten thing? Be sure to include his/her positive self-talk.
• Make a list of 5 healthy attitudes that would help anyone to "keep his/her head up" – even when rotten things happen.
• Can you make a connection to this theme? Have you ever lost a job?

When Emotions Take Over – Getting Fired from the Job

I got fired...I must be a TOTAL LOSER!

SCENARIO 24

Rory has a job that he likes and he is making pretty good money.' But, one day his boss asks him to come into the office.' His boss tells him that he has not been totally pleased' with Rory's work. Rory is then let go' from his job.

Rory is feeling extremely depressed.

 NEGATIVE THINKING

As Rory walks home from his last day on the job, negative thoughts' attack his brain.

"I **will never** get another job."

"After this, no one will **ever hire me**. I am **finished!**"

"This proves **I am a totally lousy worker**."

"My parents, my grandparents, my aunts and uncles, my friends – everyone will think I am a **loser!**"

 EMOTIONS TAKE OVER

When Rory arrives home, he goes right up to his bedroom and shuts the door. All evening he lays on the bed, reminding himself, over and over, how **horrible, rotten and terrible** it is to be fired from a job. He convinces himself, over and over, that this proves he is a **total loser.**

As time goes on, Rory becomes **more and more depressed.**

 THE UNDER-REACTION

I won't tell anyone about losing my job.

 THE OVER-REACTION

Rory then thinks: I hate my boss. I am going back to that building and spray paint' the walls with hate words.' That will teach him a lesson!

Jones is a

IN THE END...Rory has not helped himself.

Not telling people that he was fired' may save some immediate embarrassment, but this will not help him to work through this disappointment in a strong, confident way. Hiding the truth' never really helps anyone to solve a problem. And, taking revenge' on his boss is likely to get him in more trouble; this will only add to his difficulty. Both of Rory's ideas might help him to deal with his bad feelings' in the moment – but in the long run, these ideas are not healthy.

Not telling the truth' is a weak **UNDER-REACTION**. The sadness only deepens.
Spray painting the building' is a reckless **OVER-REACTION**. The sadness only deepens.

Using the S.A.T. Plan – Getting Fired from the Job

Be honest.
Be brave.
Stay positive.

Rory re-considers his two ideas. He knows that both of these ideas will not help him in the long run.' Yes, he is upset about getting fired from his job' – but he wants to deal with this unfortunate thing in a way that is honest and courageous.

Rory sits down and writes up a SAT Plan.

STOP. RELAX.

Rory begins to see something important: that his own **negative thinking** is making him more depressed' than he needs to be. He makes up his mind to think more realistically' and more positively' about what has happened. So – whenever those **depressing thoughts** begin, he tells himself:

"Stop. Relax. This is not the end of the world."

Rory then tries to look at this unfortunate thing more positively.' He begins to see that when he uses **positive self-talk** he feels less bad.'

THINK SENSIBLY. BE CALM. BE STRONG.

Rory works at changing **negative self-talk** into **positive self-talk**.
THE TRUTH IS...

"I will get another job."

"If I keep trying, someone will hire me. I am **not finished – not at all!**"

"This has **been a lesson for me. I can learn to work harder and not make mistakes**. I am a good person and I will be a better worker."

"My parents may be disappointed about this, but they will get over it. They always do. **This is not the end of the world.**"

MAKE A PLAN

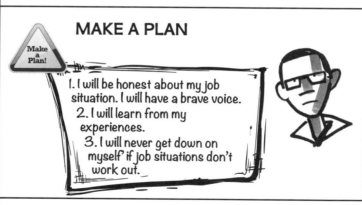

1. I will be honest about my job situation. I will have a brave voice.
2. I will learn from my experiences.
3. I will never get down on myself' if job situations don't work out.

MAKE A CONNECTION

Janine, how do you like your weekend job?

IN THE END..Rory has helped himself.

Rory realizes that it is not getting fired' that causes him to feel depressed – but it is his **own self- talk.** He knows that self-talk is **unhealthy'** when it is **unproven, untrue, exaggerated, depressing, dangerous or harmful.** He knows that self-talk is **healthy'** when it is proven, truthful, balanced, reasonable – and when it tries to look **at the positive' side** of unfortunate things. Rory is learning that: "it is not the problem – it is how I think about' the problem." And, Rory learns one other important thing about problems – talking to someone is usually helpful. **Rory's decision to solve problems using the SAT Plan is honest and courageous – just the way he wants to be!**

Practice and Share – Getting Fired from the Job

My Picture	What has happened? **OR** What might happen?
STOP. RELAX. What other self-talk could help me **avoid over-reacting** to being fired from my job?	**THINK SENSIBLY. BE CALM. BE STRONG.** What other **positive self-talk** could help me think sensibly' about this?
MAKE A PLAN	**MAKE A CONNECTION**

IN THE END...What is Likely to Happen?
Be honest. Be realistic.

Lesson Twenty-five
Not Making the Team

Ⓐ INTRODUCTION

The Social Story in Lesson Twenty-five is about Aliana. When Aliana doesn't make the team for which she tried out, she became extremely hurt, extremely angry.

Lesson Twenty-five shows that sensible thinking is the key to healthy decisions, healthy risk taking.

Ⓑ THE SCENARIO

1. Do a Guided/Shared Reading of Not Making the Team: When Emotions Take Over.
   Create a Discussion about Aliana's situation, her feelings, her reactions:
   • How is "never trying out for a team again" a "safe choice" for Aliana? How is it unhealthy?
   • How does acting out in class benefit Aliana? How is it unhealthy?

2. Now do a Guided/Shared Reading using the S.A.T. Plan.
   Create a Discussion about Aliana's reaction this time:
   • Aliana vows (to herself) to think sensibly about disappointing things. What does that mean?
   • Why is it important to congratulate ourselves for not giving up?
   • What advice would you give to Aliana?

3. Have students complete the practice page on this topic, and share their ideas with 2 or 3 others.

Ⓒ FOLLOW-UP

Suggested prompts for Journal Writing:
• Aliana has decided to never try out for a team again. Write her a letter; give her some advice.
• Aliana has decided to act out in gym class because she failed to make the team. Write her a letter; give her some advice.
• It is a good and healthy thing to sometimes take risks in life – particularly the risks that lead to your long-time happiness. What risks are worth taking? What risks are not? Write about this.

When Emotions Take Over – Not Making the Team

> I'm a lot better than some of those girls who made the team. This is HORRIBLE!

SCENARIO 25

Aliana loves basketball. She has worked hard to make the school team – not missing one practice, and practising her dribbling every night after school. On the last day of try-outs' Coach Ellen announces those players who have made the team. Aliana has failed to make the team.

Aliana is feeling very hurt and very angry.

NEGATIVE THINKING

Aliana is sitting at home, thinking about basketball – and not making the school team. "This pr**oves** that I am not as good as the others. They must be better than me. Now I look like a **real loser**."

"Coach Ellen is **totally unfair**. I worked harder than any of those other girls. She must like them better than me. I hate Coach Ellen." **"I'm a loser!"**

EMOTIONS TAKE OVER

All evening, Aliana continues to stew about not making the basketball team. Her own self-talk is focused on two things: what a **rotten a basketball player**' she must be, and what a **terribly unfair person** Coach Ellen must be.

She continues to remind herself of these two things. By the time she is ready for bed, Aliana is feeling more **hurt and angry** than ever.

THE UNDER–REACTION

Lying on her pillow, Aliana has a thought: "I am never again going to try out for a school team. Never, never, never."

THE OVER-REACTION

And just before she falls asleep, Aliana has another thought: "On Monday, I am going to act up in gym class. That will make Coach Ellen sorry that she ever cut me from the team."

IN THE END...Aliana has not helped herself.

Never again trying out for a school team is the safe way to live her life. But this decision robs her of experiences that mean a great deal to her. Acting up in class is really a cop out – it may be easier to blame Coach Ellen for this, but this decision lacks to the courage to face up to this disappointment. Both of these ideas will only deepen the problem for Aliana.

Never again trying out for a team is a pain-saving **UNDER-REACTION**.– and no long-term happiness.

Acting up in gym class' is a needless **OVER-REACTION** – and no long-term happiness.

Using the S.A.T. Plan – Not Making the Team

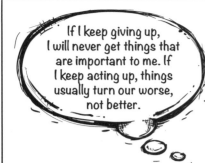 

If I keep giving up, I will never get things that are important to me. If I keep acting up, things usually turn our worse, not better.

Aliana thinks hard about her plans to deal with her failure to make the school team. And she realizes something – that both of these ideas are non solutions. These ideas don't really help her face failure with honesty and courage.

Aliana decides to make a 4-part SAT Plan.

 STOP. RELAX.

Aliana begins to examine those beliefs she has about not making the school team. She begins to understand that these mistaken beliefs are causing her to feel a great deal of hurt and anger. Whenever she thinks about her failure to make the team, she reminds herself of the first step of the SAT Plan:

"Stop. Relax. Don't over-react."

She learns to calm down, breathe deeply and to turn on her positive-thinking brain.'

 THINK SENSIBLY. BE CALM. BE STRONG.

Aliana is starting to change all of those mistaken beliefs she has about not making the team.

THE TRUTH IS...

"This might show that I may not have the skills to make this team right now. This does not make me a loser. I had the courage to work hard and try out – **good for me! I am proud of that."**

"There is **no reason to blame** Coach Ellen. I don't need to blame the coach, or anyone else, for this. This is a **disappointment** – that's all. I can learn to deal with disappointing things **without blaming** other people."

MAKE A PLAN

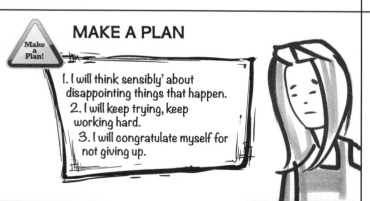

1. I will think sensibly' about disappointing things that happen.
2. I will keep trying, keep working hard.
3. I will congratulate myself for not giving up.

MAKE A CONNECTION

Dad, have you ever tried out for a team and not made it?

IN THE END..Aliana has helped herself.

Aliana is becoming more and more aware of her own mistaken beliefs about unfortunate things that happen. When she failed to make the basketball team, these mistaken beliefs' were causing her pain and anger. She believed' that failing to make the basketball team **proved that she was a loser** and that Coach Ellen was being totally unfair.' Aliana came to realize that these beliefs were silly and unproven. She started to see that failing to make a team is **only a disappointment** – and made the hurt and anger nearly disappear! As well, she made a personal connection, a talk with her dad, and that helped! **The SAT Plan helped Aliana to deal with failure courageously and honestly.**

My Picture	What has happened? **OR** What might happen?
STOP. RELAX. What other self-talk could help me **avoid over-reacting** to not making the team?	**THINK SENSIBLY. BE CALM. BE STRONG.** What other **positive self-talk** could help me think sensibly' about this?
MAKE A PLAN	**MAKE A CONNECTION**

IN THE END...What is Likely to Happen?
Be honest. Be realistic.

Lesson Twenty-six
Losing the Game

Ⓐ INTRODUCTION

The Social Story in Lesson Twenty-six is about Sonny. The "Big Game" in tennis is on the line – and Sonny is feeling very, very nervous.

Lesson Twenty-six shows that calm, strong self-coaching can alleviate extreme stress and nervousness.

Ⓑ THE SCENARIO

1. Do a Guided/Shared Reading of Losing a Game: When Emotions Take Over.
   Create a Discussion about Sonny's situation, his feelings, his reactions:
   • Why do you think that Sonny is so nervous about the upcoming game?
   • Re-read his self-talk. How does this negative thinking contribute to his extreme nervousness?

2. Now do a Guided/Shared Reading using the S.A.T. Plan.
   Create a Discussion about Sonny's reaction this time:
   • Sonny plans to stop all negative thinking (related to failure). How will he do that?
   • One of Sonny's sensible thoughts is: "It is better to think about winning." Is it? Why?
   • What other positive self-statements could Sonny use to stay focused, to stay relaxed?

3. Have students complete the practice page on this topic, and share their ideas with 2 or 3 others.

Ⓒ FOLLOW-UP

Suggested prompts for Journal Writing:
• Draw a picture of Sonny in two frames: (1) Showing self-talk that would lead to extreme nervousness; (2) showing self-talk that would lead to a focused, confident state of mind.
• List 6 self-statements that would help anyone to overcome extreme nervousness.
• List 6 things that could possibly make you very, very nervous.

When Emotions Take Over – Losing the Game

Losing that game will make me look like a FOOL!

SCENARIO 26

Sonny is a great tennis player. The big game' is on Saturday, and this will determine the top player in the whole tennis club. On Friday night, Sonny is at home thinking about the game. He knows that all of his family and friends will be watching the game. What if he loses!

Sonny is feeling very, very nervous.

NEGATIVE THINKING

As Sonny thinks about the big game' he can feel the knots in his stomach. His hands are sweating and his mouth is dry. He can only think about losing.

"I know I will lose – and I will let everyone down."

"I know I will lose – and then everyone will know that I am not so good, and they will not look up to me any more."

"I know I will lose – and I can't stand losing!"

EMOTIONS TAKE OVER

Through the evening, and even in bed, Sonny rehearses the dreadful thought of losing the big game.' He convinces himself that he will lose – and then, people will lose respect for him. He reminds himself how rotten' this would be.

By the time he is ready to fall asleep Sonny is feeling **extreme nervousness**.

THE UNDER–REACTION

Hello, Coach. Listen, I am not feeling well today. I don't think I will be able to make the big game.'

THE OVER–REACTION

Those umpires are BLIND! I should have won that game!

IN THE END...Sonny has not helped himself.

It is understandable that Sonny has some nervousness about the big game.' But his own negative self-talk has caused him to be **extremely nervous.** But his plans to deal with this nervousness does nothing to help him. Sonny's main concern is that his friends and family will somehow lose respect' for him. Will faking being sick win him more respect? Will blaming the umpire' win him more respect? No, not likely. In fact, these tricks' are likely to cause his friends and family to respect him less.

Pretending to be sick' is a cowardly **UNDER-REACTION.** Sonny's problem is still on the table.
Swearing and blaming the umpire' is a selfish **OVER-REACTION.** Sonny's problem is still on the table.

Using the S.A.T. Plan – Losing the Game

My negative self-talk is making me more nervous than I need to be.

Deep down, Sonny knows that his ideas to deal with his nervousness about the big game are ways to avoid taking responsibility for whatever happens in the tennis game tomorrow. He knows that he needs some plans to deal with the nervousness – in a way that allows him to be calm and strong.
Sonny thinks about a SAT Plan.

STOP. RELAX.

Sonny thinks about what might be causing his nervousness about the game tomorrow. He realizes that **some of those things he has been telling himself** may be causing him to be more nervous than he needs to be. When those negative thoughts come into his mind, he tells himself:

"Stop. Relax. Don't be so negative about this."

Sonny learns to calm down and relax and, especially, to think more sensibly about the possibility of losing' an important game.

THINK SENSIBLY. BE CALM. BE STRONG.

Sonny makes up his mind to **think positively and realistically** about the big game.'
THE TRUTH IS...

"If I happen to lose, I need to remember: no one **will lose respect for me**. They will probably respect me because I tried hard and did my best."

"If I happen to lose, **it's not the end of the world**. It's only one game. I may be disappointed – but I can stand it."

And another thing: "It is better to think about winning."

"I think I can win. I think I can win I think I can win."

MAKE A PLAN

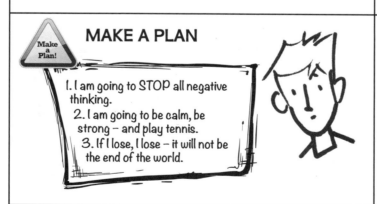

1. I am going to STOP all negative thinking.
2. I am going to be calm, be strong – and play tennis.
3. If I lose, I lose – it will not be the end of the world.

MAKE A CONNECTION

Coach, how do I control my nervousness in these important games?

IN THE END..Sonny has helped himself.

Sonny reminds himself that most people experience nervousness about an important game. Being nervous is normal. But he also realizes that his own negative thoughts are causing him to feel **more nervousness than he needs to feel.** He tries to think positive thoughts about tomorrow's game and this helps him to relax. It is a good thing for Sonny when he connects with his tennis coach. The coach helps him to **think** more positively about the game, to **focus on winning** – but, also, to be courageous in defeat. The coach reminds Sonny that this is only a game. **Sonny's SAT Plan has helped him to manage his extreme nervousness in these tense situations.**

Practice and Share – Losing the Game

My Picture	What has happened? **OR** What might happen?
STOP. RELAX. What other self-talk could help me **avoid over-reacting** to losing a game?	**THINK SENSIBLY. BE CALM. BE STRONG.** What other **positive self-talk** could help me think sensibly' about this?
MAKE A PLAN	**MAKE A CONNECTION**

IN THE END...What is Likely to Happen?
Be honest. Be realistic.

Lesson Twenty-seven
Losing a Talent Contest

Ⓐ INTRODUCTION

The Social Story in Lesson Twenty-seven is about Zoë. Zoë wants to take part in the local talent contest, but whenever she thinks about it, she becomes extremely nervous.

Lesson Twenty-seven shows how personal commitments to remain calm and strong in the face of stressful events (often) lead to successful outcomes.

Ⓑ THE SCENARIO

1. Do a Guided/Shared Reading of Losing a Talent Contest: When Emotions Take Over.
   Create a Discussion about Zoë's situation, her feelings, her reactions:
   • Pessimism is an attitude that expects the worst. How is Zoë's attitude pessimistic?
   • Which do you think is unhealthier: Zoë's under-reaction or her over-reaction?

2. Now do a Guided/Shared Reading using the S.A.T. Plan.
   Create a Discussion about Zoë's reaction this time:
   • Optimism is an attitude that expects the best. How is Zoë's attitude optimistic?
   • Re-read Zoë's sensible thinking. Which one do you think is the most effective?
   • Re-read Zoë's plan. How is this plan optimistic?

3. Have students complete the practice page on this topic, and share their ideas with 2 or 3 others.

Ⓒ FOLLOW-UP

Suggested prompts for Journal Writing:
• Draw a scene of Zoë trying out for the talent contest. Be sure to add her self-talk.
• Make a list of 8 optimistic self-statements.
• Make a personal connection to Zoë's story. How did you feel? Will you ever try that again?

When Emotions Take Over – Losing a Talent Contest

SCENARIO 27

Zoë is a very good guitar player. Should she complete in the Citywide Talent Show that is coming up? Zoë thinks about performing in front of her family and friends, and it scares her. When Zoë thinks about the possibility of losing the talent show, she becomes **extremely anxious.**

 ### NEGATIVE THINKING

"Should I sign up for the talent contest?" Zoë wonders? Her hands begin to shake – and her mind is filled with negative pictures.

"I **will make mistakes** – and my friends will laugh at me."

"I **will make mistakes** – and my family will be embarrassed."

"I **make mistakes** – and that is horrible, terrible, rotten."

 ### EMOTIONS TAKE OVER

All weekend, Zoë wonders if she should take part in the Citywide Talent Show, and all weekend she pictures only negative images in her mind – making mistakes; losing the contest; her friends laughing; her parents leaving in embarrassment.

With all of these negative pictures' in her mind, it is no wonder that Zoë feels **extremely anxious.**

THE UNDER–REACTION

I'm going to leave that guitar in its case.

THE OVER–REACTION

Most of those players sound like a bunch of monkeys trying to make music.

IN THE END...Zoë has not helped herself.

It is quite normal that Zoë is a little anxious about the talent show. But those negative pictures in her mind are causing her to be **extremely anxious**. Zoë has two ideas to lessen her fear of failure – yet, both of these ideas are not really in her best interests. By choosing not to participate in the talent show, she may be losing out in something that could help her grow as a guitar player, and by choosing to make fun of the other performers she will likely lose respect for herself and others.

Not taking part in the show is an easy-way-out **UNDER-REACTION** – and Zoë has not grown.
Making fun of the other performers' is a silly **OVER-REACTION** – and Zoë has not grown.

Using the S.A.T. Plan – Losing a Talent Contest

Zoë thinks about her two choices. She is beginning to see that negative plans do not really help her – she wants to lessen her own anxiousness. She wants to face her fear of failure' with honesty and courage.

Zoë wants to take a risk.' She sits down and carefully designs a 4-part Sensible Acting & Thinking Plan.

 STOP. RELAX.

Zoë is beginning to understand that those negative pictures are causing her great anxiety about the talent show. The next time she thinks about herself on the stage of the talent show, she tells herself:

"Stop. Relax. Be positive."

Zoë is getting better and better at stopping those negative pictures. She is getting better and better at relaxing herself' and staying positive.

 THINK SENSIBLY. BE CALM. BE STRONG.

Zoë knows that negative pictures bring unproven, unhealthy ideas.
THE TRUTH IS...

"If I make a few mistakes – my friends will still like and respect me."

"If I make a few mistakes – my family will be happy that I took a chance."

"Making a mistake is **not the end of the world.**"

"I probably **won't make mistakes** anyway."

MAKE A PLAN

MAKE A CONNECTION

IN THE END..Zoë has helped herself.

Zoë is learning to be **more realistic** about making mistakes. She works at changing those negative pictures' into more **sensible, positive pictures**. She actively reminds herself that her friends and her family will be hoping for her. She reminds herself **that making mistakes and not winning the competition are things that she can deal with**. Zoë connects with her sister about this, and this helps her to feel safe, stay positive, and not become so anxious about this. **Zoë's SAT Plan has helped her to stay positive about the possibility of not winning the talent show.**

Practice and Share – Losing a Talent Contest

My Picture	What has happened? **OR** What might happen?
![STOP Relax] **STOP. RELAX.** What other self-talk could help me **avoid over-reacting** to maybe losing a talent show?	![Be Strong Be CALM] **THINK SENSIBLY. BE CALM. BE STRONG.** What other **positive self-talk** could help me think sensibly' about this?
![Make a Plan] **MAKE A PLAN**	![Make a Connection] **MAKE A CONNECTION**

IN THE END...What is Likely to Happen?
Be honest. Be realistic.

Lesson Twenty-eight
Losing a Race

Ⓐ INTRODUCTION

The Social Story in Lesson Twenty-eight is about Cameron. When Cameron failed to win the race at the local track meet, he became quite depressed.

Lesson Twenty-eight shows how negative views contribute to under-and-over reactions.

Ⓑ THE SCENARIO

1. Do a Guided/Shared Reading of Losing the Race: When Emotions Take Over.
   Create a Discussion about Cameron's situation, his feelings, his reactions:
   • Re-examine Cameron's self-talk. Does he take a positive or negative view of not winning?
   • How does this view contribute to what he decides to do?

2. Now do a Guided/Shared Reading using the S.A.T. Plan.
   Create a Discussion about Cameron's reaction this time:
   • Re-examine Cameron's new self-talk. Does he take a positive or negative view of not winning?
   • How does this new view contribute to what he decides to do?
   • Re-read Cameron's plan. What else might he have done (as an appropriate reaction)?

3. Have students complete the practice page on this topic, and share their ideas with 2 or 3 others.

Ⓒ FOLLOW-UP

Suggested prompts for Journal Writing:
• Write a short story about "The Big Race". Show how the main character deals with "coming in dead last" in a positive, successful way. Be sure to show her/his view.
• Make a list of 5 helpful, healthy viewpoints that any racer should use.
• Make a personal connection to Cameron's story. How did you feel? Will you ever race again?

When Emotions Take Over – Losing a Race

> Second place is totally HORRIBLE!

SCENARIO 28

Cameron is on the school track team, and he has been training for months. He wanted to be the fastest boy on the entire track team. In today's track meet, Cameron came in second. Whenever Cameron thinks about losing the race, he becomes depressed.

 NEGATIVE THINKING

Cameron hates the walk to school. He thinks about all the comments he will get today. He lost the race and negative thoughts are now filling his head.

"I came in second place – **that is horrible**!"

"People **won't look up to me** anymore – I can't stand this!"

"All that training was **for nothing**."

"**I am a loser**."

 EMOTIONS TAKE OVER

Cameron is filling his own head with exaggerated, unproven, gloomy notions. He convinces himself that coming in second in the race is a **horrible, rotten thing**. Worse than that, he convinces himself that he has **lost the respect** of his friends at school – and that he must now be a loser.

By the time he gets to school, Cameron is feeling more depressed than ever.

THE UNDER-REACTION

> I don't want to see any of my friends. I'm staying home all day!

THE OVER-REACTION

Cameron has a second thought: "If anybody mentions that race, I will punch him in the head."

IN THE END...Cameron has not helped himself.

Is losing the race causing Cameron to feel depressed? If it did, then losing races would make everyone feel depressed. Clearly, that is not the case – there are many people who lose races, yet do not get depressed. Cameron's **feelings of depression** are more directly related to his **negative beliefs** about losing the race. He somehow believes that coming in second must mean that people will **no longer respect him** – and that this must make him a **loser**. Losing a race will likely be disappointing for anyone, but if someone attaches **very negative, exaggerated, mistaken beliefs** to losing a race, that person is likely to become **depressed**.

Skipping school is a short-term **UNDER-REACTION** – and Cameron's problem just gets bigger.
Punching someone in the face is a silly **OVER-REACTION** – and Cameron's problem just gets bigger.

Using the S.A.T. Plan – Losing a Race

My EMOTIONAL brain leads me to give up OR to get angry. I need to turn on my THINKING brain.

Cameron thinks about his idea to skip school and his idea to punch someone who might mention his failure to win the race. He quickly realizes that these are cowardly reactions of his own emotional brain.

Cameron puts his thinking brain in control. He goes to school and that evening works out a SAT Plan.

STOP. RELAX.

Cameron begins to see that his own negative beliefs are causing him to become depressed about losing the race. When those negative beliefs come into his mind, he tells himself: **"Stop. Relax. Don't get depressed about this."**

Cameron is learning that simply by telling himself to relax, calm down, and to stay positive, he is able to better control his own feelings.

THINK SENSIBLY. BE CALM. BE STRONG.

Cameron sees that his old beliefs about losing the race are overly exaggerated and overly negative.

THE TRUTH IS...

"Coming in second in the race is **disappointing** – but **it's not that bad**."

"Some of my friends might talk to me about the race – that's okay, **I can handle that**."

"All that training was **good for me**."

"I am proud that I work hard as a runner."

MAKE A PLAN

1. I will talk openly about coming in second.
2. I will be proud that I tried hard.
3. I will be calm, strong, open and honest.

MAKE A CONNECTION

Having an open, honest talk with his father is part of being CALM and STRONG.

IN THE END..Cameron has helped himself.

Cameron is learning to **question** his own exaggerated, negative beliefs. If he chooses to believe that coming in second in the race is horrible, terrible, rotten – then it becomes that. On the other hand, if he chooses to believe that coming in second is only disappointing – then it becomes that. Cameron is actively changing his exaggerated, mistaken beliefs. When he is able to do this, he may feel **a little disappointed – but never depressed**. And, by **talking to his dad**, he feels much better. **Cameron's Sensible Acting & Thinking Plan has helped him to be reasonable about disappointing things.**

Practice and Share – Losing a Race

My Picture	What has happened? **OR** What might happen?
STOP. RELAX. What other self-talk could help me **avoid over-reacting** to a feeling of losing a race.	**THINK SENSIBLY. BE CALM. BE STRONG.** What other **positive self-talk** could help me think sensibly' about this?
MAKE A PLAN	**MAKE A CONNECTION**

IN THE END...What is Likely to Happen?
Be honest. Be realistic.

Lesson Twenty-nine
Pet Dying

Ⓐ INTRODUCTION

The Social Story in Lesson Twenty-eight is about Lorna. When Lorna discovers that her cat, Tabi, has died, she becomes extremely depressed – and she is convinced she will be sad forever.

Lesson Twenty-nine shows that dealing with very sad events in life is helped by a balanced, healthy view of what has happened.

Ⓑ THE SCENARIO

1. Do a Guided/Shared Reading of Pet Dying: When Emotions Take Over.
   Create a Discussion about Lorna's situation, her feelings, her reactions:
   • Re-examine Lorna's under-reaction. What do you think of her decision?
   • Re-examine Lorna's over-reaction. What do you think of her decision?

2. Now do a Guided/Shared Reading using the S.A.T. Plan.
   Create a Discussion about Lorna's reaction this time:
   • Lorna has decided to view her pet's life and death differently. What do think about this view?
   • How does this new view contribute to what she decides to do?
   • Re-read Lorna's plan. Is this a balanced, healthy plan? How so?

3. Have students complete the practice page on this topic, and share their ideas with 2 or 3 others.

Ⓒ FOLLOW-UP

Suggested prompts for Journal Writing:
• Write a letter to Lorna. How would you help her to deal with the loss of her pet?
• If you can, make a personal connection to this story.
• Do a mini-poster: Coping with the loss of a pet. Include helpful self-talk about this.

SCENARIO 29

When Lorna comes home from school, her mother has bad news. Lorna's beautiful pet cat, Tabi, has died. Lorna cannot believe it! Tabi has been very special to her, and now she is gone. "How will I ever get over this?" she wonders.

Lorna feels extremely depressed.

NEGATIVE THINKING

Lorna does not go to school the next day. She lies in bed, thinking about Tabi. She cries and cries, and whenever she thinks about living without her little pet, she becomes more depressed.

"It is **totally unfair** that Tabi has died."

"I **will never** get over this."

"There can never **be another pet like Tabi**."

"This is the worst thing that could ever happen to me."

EMOTIONS TAKE OVER

As Lorna lies in bed, she keeps reminding herself of the unfairness of Tabi's death. She keeps reminding herself that this is a horrible, horrible thing – and something she will never get over.

More depressed than ever, Lorna cries herself to sleep.

THE UNDER–REACTION

No more pets ever...I will just be hurt again.

THE OVER-REACTION

I don't want to talk about it! Just mind your own business!

IN THE END...Lorna has not helped herself.

Is Lorna dealing with the loss of her pet in a healthy, successful way? Her idea to never have another pet may protect her from some hurt (when the pet dies), but this plan also robs her of the real joy that a pet can add to her life. Her idea to scream at her friends if they should mention her pet's name is not really going to help her **deal with her sadness,** and it is an idea that is **unfair to her friends**. Lorna needs to deal with this very sad event - in a way that helps her to **accept this loss and to move on and to be fair to others.**

 Never getting another pet is a needless **UNDER-REACTION** – and her sadness continues. Screaming at her friends is a useless, unfair **OVER-REACTION** – and her sadness continues.

Using the S.A.T. Plan – Pet Dying

I don't think Tabi would want me to be sad forever. I am going to look at things a little differently.

Lorna knows that it is normal and understandable to feel very sad when a pet dies. But, she wonders: "Am I dealing with this sadness in a healthy, successful way?"

Lorna knows that she must accept Tabi's death and she must learn to move on. Lorna sits down and creates a SAT Plan.

STOP. RELAX.

Lorna understands that Tabi's death is a sad thing. But, she suspects that some of her self-talk may not be helping her to **accept this and to move on.** When the negative, gloomy self-talk comes into her mind, she tells herself:

"Stop. Relax. Think happy thoughts about Tabi."

Lorna learns to help herself by focusing on happy, positive thoughts about her pet's life.

THINK SENSIBLY. BE CALM. BE STRONG.

Lorna decides to help herself with positive self-talk about Tabi's death:
THE TRUTH IS...

"Tabi is gone – and now I am going to **remember her with a smile**. I will think about all of the fun times that we had. I think that Tabi would want me to accept that she is gone, and to move on."

"I will learn get over this."

"There will never be another pet like Tabi – but that is okay."

MAKE A PLAN

Every time I look at Tabi's picture I am going to think about all the good times – and I will smile.

MAKE A CONNECTION

Stacey, have you ever had a favorite pet die? Do you think I should get another pet?

IN THE END..Lorna has helped herself.

When Lorna finds out that her pet has died, she is very sad – and that is normal and understandable. But, as time goes on, she realizes that she has a choice about how to think about Tabi. She can remind herself how **terrible, rotten, and unfair** it is that Tabi has died. Or, she can think about the many happy memories Tabi has left. She can remember Tabi with great sadness, or she can remember Tabi with a **smile**. Lorna chooses to think positive thoughts about her pet. Also, she finds that talking to her best friend, Stacey, helps her to accept Tabi's death and to move on. **Lorna's SAT Plan has helped her to think positive thoughts – even when something rotten happens!**

Practice and Share – Pet Dying

My Picture	What has happened? **OR** What might happen?
STOP. RELAX. What other self-talk could help me **avoid over-reacting** to a pet dying?	**THINK SENSIBLY. BE CALM. BE STRONG.** What other **positive self-talk** could help me think sensibly' about this?
MAKE A PLAN	**MAKE A CONNECTION**

IN THE END...What is Likely to Happen?
Be honest. Be realistic.

Lesson Thirty
Parents Not Getting Along

Ⓐ INTRODUCTION

The Social Story in Lesson Thirty is about William. When William sees and hears his parents not getting along, he feels extremely helpless, guilty and frightened.

Lesson Thirty shows that it is possible to deal with unfortunate events in life by adopting a healthy, rational outlook and a positive, workable plan of action.

Ⓑ THE SCENARIO

1. Do a Guided/Shared Reading of Parents Not Getting Along: When Emotions Take Over.
   Create a Discussion about William's situation, his feelings, his reactions:
   • William convinces himself that his parents' arguing must be his fault. Is this true and provable?
   • William convinces himself that if his parents get a divorce, he will never be happy again. Is this true and provable?

2. Now do a Guided/Shared Reading using the S.A.T. Plan.
   Create a Discussion about William's reaction this time:
   • Look again at William's sensible thinking. What do think about this view?
   • How does this new view contribute to what he decides to do?
   • Re-read William's 4-part plan. What other ideas do you have for William?

3. Have students complete the practice page on this topic, and share their ideas with 2 or 3 others.

Ⓒ FOLLOW-UP

Suggested prompts for Journal Writing:
• Write a letter to William. Give him the best advice you can?
• Write 5 sensible, positive self-statements that would help William with this rotten thing.
• Draw William with his parents – with dialogue from each of them.

When Emotions Take Over – Parents Not Getting Along

All of this must be my fault!

William knows that his parents have not been getting along. And, it seems to be getting worse. Last night they were arguing loudly – and William heard it all from his room. He wonders what will happen to his family. William feels helpless and guilty and frightened.

NEGATIVE THINKING

After hearing another mom-and-dad argument, William lies in bed. **Negative thoughts** and **negative pictures** seem to be worse at night:

"My parents are unhappy, and it must be my fault."

"My parents will get a divorce, and that will be **horrible, horrible, horrible. I won't be able to deal with that** and I **will never be happy again**."

"Mom **will never be happy**. Dad **will never be happy**. Our family is **ruined**. We will all be **miserable for the rest of our lives**."

EMOTIONS TAKE OVER

William's mind is invaded by negative thoughts and negative pictures. These thoughts and pictures remind him, over and over, of the worst things that will happen as a result of his parents arguing. He convinces himself that this must be his fault and that these arguments will end in misery for his whole family.

William believes that he is to blame for all of this. H**e feels guilty.** He believes that there is nothing he can do to change the situation. **He feels helpless and frightened**. He believes that there is no escaping the endless misery of this.

THE UNDER-REACTION

I'm going to pretend this is not happening.

THE OVER-REACTION

I'm going to run far away...That will teach them a lesson!

IN THE END...William has not helped himself.

William is faced with a personal hardship that would be truly difficult for anyone to face. It is understandable that he is feeling frightened and helpless. But his idea to ignore his parents and to pretend that this is not happening is only putting the problem in the closet - sooner or later he needs to deal with this unfortunate issue. His second idea, to run away from home, is a desperate plan to show his parents how upset and angry he is – but, running away will not help him to deal with this issue in the long run.

Ignoring his parents is a do-nothing **UNDER-REACTION**. The feelings of helplessness are still there. Running away is a dramatic **OVER-REACTION**. The feelings of helplessness are still there.

Using the S.A.T. Plan – Parents Not Getting Along

> I can learn to deal with this sad thing in my life.

William reminds himself he has to face a difficult personal issue – something that would be difficult for anyone! He asks himself: "How do I deal with this sad situation in a healthy, thoughtful way?"

He decides to face this problem as bravely and smartly as he can. William gets a pencil and paper and makes up a SAT Plan.

 ## STOP. RELAX.

William knows that having to live with arguing parents is not easy. Yet, he is beginning to realize that those gloomy thoughts and pictures are causing him to feel guiltier, more helpless, and more frightened than he needs to.

When the negative thoughts and pictures start to come, he stops them cold. He tells himself:

"Stop. Relax. This is not totally rotten. I can learn to deal with this."

Over time, William learns to help himself by reminding himself that he is strong and thoughtful – and that he can deal with this sad event.

 ## THINK SENSIBLY. BE CALM. BE STRONG.

William does not let the negative thoughts and pictures make the situation worse.
THE TRUTH IS...

"Yes, my parents are arguing – **but this is not my fault**."

"My parents might be going through a difficult time, but **this may pass**. But, if they do get a divorce, **that does not need to be horrible. I can learn to deal with that**. Mom can learn to be happy and so can Dad. Our family situation will change, but it is **not ruined**. My parents may not get divorced – but if that happened, I will be okay."

MAKE A PLAN

> First, I will remind myself that this is an unfortunate thing. (It is only HORRIBLE if I tell myself so.) Second, I can talk to my parents and help to make the best of this for everyone.

MAKE A CONNECTION

> William's talk with his mom and dad was not easy – but it helped everyone to be open and honest about their feelings.

IN THE END..William has helped himself.

William is helping himself to deal with an unfortunate family problem. He realizes that the **most helpful** thing he can do is to **change the way he thinks** about his parents arguing. He does not allow those gloomy thoughts and pictures to deepen his feelings of guilt, helplessness and fright. He thinks more reasonably about the arguments – and even about the possibility of divorce. William is learning to deal with this sad event in **a brave, thoughtful way**. One day, he makes an **important connection**: he is able to have a **calm, honest talk** with his parents about his, and that makes him feel much better. **William's SAT Plan is helping him to be calm and strong and positive – even when a rotten thing happens!**

Practice and Share – Parents Not Getting Along

My Picture	What has happened? **OR** What might happen?
STOP. RELAX. What other self-talk could help me **avoid overreacting** to my parents arguing?	**THINK SENSIBLY. BE CALM. BE STRONG.** What other **positive self-talk** could help me think sensibly' about this?
MAKE A PLAN	**MAKE A CONNECTION**

IN THE END...What is Likely to Happen?
Be honest. Be realistic.

Lesson Thirty-one
Getting Sick

Ⓐ INTRODUCTION

The Social Story in Lesson Thirty-one is about Wauneta. When Wauneta discovers that she must go to the hospital and receive treatment for an illness, she becomes very, very worried.

Lesson Thirty-one shows that in the face of an unavoidable rotten event, dire, gloomy self-talk is sure to amplify worry, while positive, balanced self-talk is sure to diminish worry.

Ⓑ THE SCENARIO

1. Do a Guided/Shared Reading of Getting Sick: When Emotions Take Over.
    Create a Discussion about Wauneta's situation, her feelings, her reactions:
    • How is Wauneta actually making her unfortunate illness even worse?
    • Wauneta tells herself over and over that her parents "won't be able to handle" her sickness. This is the "belief system" that she has chosen. Is this belief necessarily true?

2. Now do a Guided/Shared Reading using the S.A.T. Plan.
    Create a Discussion about Wauneta's reaction this time:
    • Wauneta actively chooses a different belief system about her unfortunate situation. How so?
    • What do you think is her most positive belief about her illness – the one that will help her most?
    • Re-read Wauneta's 4-part plan. Could she have added anything else?

3. Have students complete the practice page on this topic, and share their ideas with 2 or 3 others.

Ⓒ FOLLOW-UP

Suggested prompts for Journal Writing:
• Write a self-help column entitled, "Thinking Positively about Your Illness."
• Create a poster that might be hung in a hospital – helping people not to worry about sickness.
• Draw Wauneta at home, thinking more positively about her unfortunate illness – be sure to include her positive, sensible beliefs.

When Emotions Take Over – Getting Sick

I don't know what will happen to me. I am so WORRIED!

SCENARIO 31

Before she went to the doctor, Wauneta was not feeling well. Now, she must go to the hospital for treatment. She is not sure how long the treatment will last, but she must stay in the hospital for several days. Wauneta is **very worried** – for herself and for her parents.

 ## NEGATIVE THINKING

Wauneta must go into the hospital tomorrow. Tonight, her self-talk is filled with worry:

"What if I **never get better**? Oh no, oh no, oh no."

"I will miss school and **I will fail**. That would be **horrible, horrible, horrible**."

"**I can't stand** feeling sick!"

"**I can't stand** any pain!"

"My parents **won't be able to deal** with this!"

 ## EMOTIONS TAKE OVER

Wauneta has many dark, negative pictures in her mind. She sees herself lying the hospital, experiencing nothing but pain and misery. Her focus is on the worst things that might happen: that she will not get better and that she will fail her school year and that the sickness and pain will be too much for her to bear. She convinces herself that her parents will not be able to deal with this. As her self-talk becomes darker and more negative, **Wauneta feels more and more worried.**

 ## THE UNDER-REACTION

I am going to keep my worry inside of me.

THE OVER-REACTION

GET AWAY from me!

IN THE END...Wauneta has not helped herself.

It is easy to understand the **feelings of worry** that Wauneta is having. Going into the hospital and missing school would create a certain amount of worry in anyone. Rather than not worrying at all, Wauneta might try to **worry less.** It is normal to be concerned about her sickness and about missing school – but not to become **extremely upset. Hiding her worry** from Mom and Dad and friends will not help, and **yelling and screaming and running away** will not help. Those plans will not make her worry any less.

Not talking about her worries is a painful **UNDER-REACTION.** The worry is still there.
Telling others to get away is a dramatic **OVER-REACTION.** The worry is still there.

Using the S.A.T. Plan – Getting Sick

Wauneta thinks about going to the hospital – and she thinks about her constant worrying. Finally, she decides that it is time to be as brave as she can and to be a little less worried about what she has to do.

Wauneta turns on her thinking brain and creates a Sensible Acting & Thinking Plan.

 STOP. RELAX.

Wauneta is beginning to understand something important: **there are some things we cannot change – and the best thing to do is to accept things and try to worry less.** When those worry-thoughts come into her head, she tells herself:

 "Stop. Relax. Going into the hospital is not fun, but it is not totally horrible. I can be calm and strong about this."

Slow**ly but surely Wauneta learns to** think sensibly about her sickness. She reminds herself that she can manage whatever happens.

 THINK SENSIBLY. BE CALM. BE STRONG.

Wauneta refuses to let those worry-thoughts get her down. She begins to realize that many of those thoughts are exaggerated, unproven and needlessly gloomy.
THE TRUTH IS...

 "I am not going to focus on being sick; **I am going to focus on getting better.**"
"I'll talk to my teachers and I will make a plan about school. I don't need to worry about that."
"Being sick is not fun – but I **can handle this**!"
"It may not be easy – but I can stand the pain!"
"My parents **will be concerned – but they will be able to deal with this**!"

 MAKE A PLAN

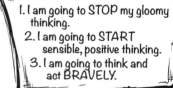

1. I am going to STOP my gloomy thinking.
2. I am going to START sensible, positive thinking.
3. I am going to think and act BRAVELY.

MAKE A CONNECTION

Jimmi, I have to go into the hospital and it's a bit scary for me.

IN THE END..Wauneta has helped herself.
Wauneta is learning to **manage her own worry-thoughts**. By **thinking differently** about the rotten thing that has happened to her, it becomes less rotten. She now **watches what she tells herself** – and she does not accept any **self-talk that is unproven or exaggerated or overly gloomy**. She makes a **positive plan** to face her sickness as strongly as she can. And she makes a **connection**: by telling her best friend about her worries, she feels better. It is so much better when she can **be honest** about her own feelings. **Wauneta's SAT Plan helps her to lessen her own worries and to deal with this unfortunate sickness as honestly and bravely as she can.**

Practice and Share – Getting Sick

My Picture	What has happened? **OR** What might happen?
STOP. RELAX. What other self-talk could help me **avoid over-reacting** to an illness?	**THINK SENSIBLY. BE CALM. BE STRONG.** What other **positive self-talk** could help me think sensibly' about this?
MAKE A PLAN	**MAKE A CONNECTION**

IN THE END...What is Likely to Happen?
Be honest. Be realistic.

Lesson Thirty-two
Having to Move

Ⓐ INTRODUCTION

The Social Story in Lesson Thirty-two is about James. James finds out that his father has transferred to a new job location and his family is now moving. He feels very frustrated and hateful.

Lesson Thirty-two shows that rigid, negative attitudes to an unavoidable event often ignite the Emotional Brain – along with under-and-over reactions.

Ⓑ THE SCENARIO

1. Do a Guided/Shared Reading of Moving: When Emotions Take Over.
    Create a Discussion about James's situation, his feelings, his reactions:
    • James describes his having to move as "horrible, terrible, rotten." Is it necessarily so?
    • James convinces himself that he will never be happy again. Is it necessarily so?

2. Now do a Guided/Shared Reading using the S.A.T. Plan.
    Create a Discussion about James's reaction this time:
    • James plans to be less emotional about the move. How does he do this?
    • James begins to look at the bright side of moving. How does he do this?
    • James vows to "make the best" of having to move. How might he do that?

3. Have students complete the practice page on this topic, and share their ideas with 2 or 3 others.

Ⓒ FOLLOW-UP

Suggested prompts for Journal Writing:
• Write a list of "5 good things about having to move."
• Draw side-by-side pictures of James – one, with negative thoughts about moving; two with positive thoughts about moving.
• Have you ever had to move from one home to another? Write about that experience.

When Emotions Take Over – Having to Move

SCENARIO 32

On Tuesday, James' father came home from work and told the family that his job had changed. That night, the family had a long discussion and a decision was made: they would move to a new city. James did not agree with the decision. He feels **very frightened, very hateful.**

 ## NEGATIVE THINKING

For the next several days James can only think about the family's move. Every thought is negative and full of sadness.

"I will miss my friends, and that is going to be **horrible, terrible, rotten**."

"I will **never be happy** in our new place."

"I will have to start all over – and **I won't be able to do that**."

"Mom and Dad are being terribly unfair – **I hate them for that**!"

 ## EMOTIONS TAKE OVER

In his own mind, James can think of nothing good about moving to a new city. He is stuck like glue on the notion that moving will be "the most rotten thing in the world." Every thought about the move is glum and negative – and, in a few days James is able to convince himself that "he will never be happy again."

James refuses to accept the move. His self-talk is totally negative. He feels **frustrated** by the plan to move, and **hateful** towards his parents.

THE UNDER–REACTION

I won't talk to them. I won't help them. I will do nothing at all!

THE OVER-REACTION

I will refuse to move! I am NOT moving! No way! No way!

IN THE END...James has not helped himself.

It is not uncommon to feel badly at having to move. It is not easy to leave friends and home behind. James has two ideas that he thinks will help him to express all of the **frustration and hatred** that have built up inside his mind: he will be **totally uncooperative** in the move, or he will throw wild temper tantrums. In truth, both of these plans are likely to make his personal situation **worse than ever**. Both of these ideas will only **add to the tension** in his family – and, chances are, he will still have to move!

Not cooperating with his family is a stubborn **UNDER-REACTION**. The problem is still there.
Saying he will not move is a tension-building **OVER-REACTION**. The problem is still there.

Using the S.A.T. Plan – Having to Move

James begins to re-think his plan to not cooperate or to throw temper tantrums. He finally admits to himself: these actions won't help me or my family. I need to be less emotional about this, and to be more intelligent.

James gets smart. He writes up a 4-part SAT Plan.

 STOP. RELAX.

As the days pass, it becomes clear to James: **what I cannot change, I need to make the best of.** He works at changing the negative self-talk that is causing his feelings of frustration and hatred. When the negative thoughts come to his mind, he tells himself:

"Stop. Relax. Make the best of this."

James works hard to think positively about the family's move. The more he practices, the better he gets – and the better he feels.

He thinks about the positive aspects of moving.

 THINK SENSIBLY. BE CALM. BE STRONG.

When James thinks about all of his negative self-talk about moving, he realizes that these ideas are overly negative and not necessarily true.

THE TRUTH IS...

"Yes, I will miss my friends – **but that is okay.** I can still keep in touch."

"I will **make new friends and be just as happy** in our new place."

"I will have to start all over – **but that's okay.** I am strong and confident. I just need to **be patient."**

"Mom and Dad are **not trying to be unfair – I am trying to understand that!"**

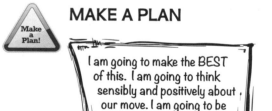 **MAKE A PLAN**

I am going to make the BEST of this. I am going to think sensibly and positively about our move. I am going to be calm strong and patient.

 **MAKE A CONNECTION**

Don, I have to move but we can stay in touch thorugh email.

IN THE END..James has helped himself.

James works out a **SAT Plan** that helps him to **accept** the fact that his family has to move. Most importantly, the plan gives him a sense of **hope for the future** and a **plan of action**. Instead of moping around the **house and feeling frustrated and hateful, he is trying to make this change** as positive as he can. One day he wonders to himself: **Who knows – maybe I will like this new place even better!** He has a talk with his best friend, Don, and they decide to stay in touch by phone and email. **James' SAT Plan is helping him to be strong, be positive – and to accept things he cannot change.**

Practice and Share – Having to Move

My Picture	What has happened? **OR** What might happen?
STOP. RELAX. What other self-talk could help me **avoid over-reacting** to moving away?	**THINK SENSIBLY. BE CALM. BE STRONG.** What other **positive self-talk** could help me think sensibly' about this?
MAKE A PLAN	**MAKE A CONNECTION**

IN THE END...What is Likely to Happen?
Be honest. Be realistic.

Lesson Thirty-three
Dad Losing His Job

Ⓐ INTRODUCTION

The Social Story in Lesson Thirty-three is about Shim. When Shim finds out that her father has lost his job, she becomes very frightened, very worried.

Lesson Thirty-three shows that worry and fright are amplified by dire, exaggerated self-talk.

Ⓑ THE SCENARIO

1. Do a Guided/Shared Reading of Dad Losing His Job: When Emotions Take Over.
   Create a Discussion about Shim's situation, her feelings, her reactions:
   • Why would Shim choose to keep this totally to herself? How does that help her worry less?
   • Why would Shim choose to yell and swear at others (for finding out her dad lost his job)?

2. Now do a Guided/Shared Reading using the S.A.T. Plan.
   Create a Discussion about Shim's reaction this time:
   • How have Shim's self-statements changed?
   • How have Shim's plans changed?
   • What would make Shim's plan tricky or difficult? Do you think she will be successful?

3. Have students complete the practice page on this topic, and share their ideas with 2 or 3 others.

Ⓒ FOLLOW-UP

Suggested prompts for Journal Writing:
• Write a secret note to Shim. Help her deal with her dilemma.
• Can you make any connection to the story? Has anyone you know had to change jobs? How did you deal with that?
• Sometimes rotten things turn out better than ever. Write a story about a character that lost her/his job – but things became even better than before.

When Emotions Take Over – Dad Losing His Job

"Dad lost his job. We will lose EVERYTHING! This is HORRIBLE!"

SCENARIO 33

It is a sad day for Shim and her family. Shim's father has informed them that today he lost his job. He would now have to start looking for other work. When the announcement is made, Shim does not say anything. Yet, she feels **very frightened, very worried**.

NEGATIVE THINKING

At school, Shim is very quiet. It is hard for her to focus on her school work, and she does not talk much to her friends. Her mind is filled with worry thoughts.

"My dad might **never** find another job."

"We might **lose our house**. We might **lose our car**. We might **have to move**."

"My parents might **start arguing** about this."

"This is **horrible, rotten, terrible** – we might **never be happy again**!"

EMOTIONS TAKE OVER

Shim's worry thoughts have taken over. Her self-talk is focused on the terribleness of this unexpected event. She imagines the very worst of things: losing their home and their money – and their happiness.

At school, one negative thought builds on another. By the end of school each day, Shim is feeling very **frightened, very worried.**

THE UNDER–REACTION

I am going to keep this totally to myself!

THE OVER-REACTION

If anyone says anything, I will yell and swear at them... That will make them stop!

IN THE END...Shim has not helped herself.

Shim and her family must deal with an **unexpected and unhappy event**. Shim has two thoughts on how she might deal with her own feelings. Choosing to **suffer in silence** will not in any way lessen her feelings of worry and fright. Also, **yelling and swearing** at her friends will only end up making her feel **more alone, more frightened and more worried**. Clearly, Shim needs a new idea, a new plan.

Not talking to anyone about this is a quiet **UNDER-REACTION**. The stress and worry only build. Yelling and swearing at her friends is a frantic **OVER-REACTION**. The stress and worry only build.

Shim knows that her family is feeling sad about Dad losing his job. But she wonders if her own worry thoughts are making this unfortunate thing even worse. She makes up her mind to worry less about this – and to face up to this bravely and openly.

Shim creates a helpful SAT Plan.

STOP. RELAX.

Shim realizes something very important: worrying does not really help things. While it is often helpful to **be concerned** about things in our lives, it **rarely helps to worry-worry-worry** about those things. Shim pays attention to her own worry-thoughts and when she hears them coming, she tells herself:

"Stop. Relax. Worrying does not help."

Shim is getting better at controlling her own worry-thoughts. As she examines them, she realizes that these thoughts are often **exaggerated, unproven, overly gloomy, overly negative – and pretty much useless.**

THINK SENSIBLY. BE CALM. BE STRONG.

Next, Shim works at changing her unproven, gloomy, negative self-talk into logical, positive self-talk.

THE TRUTH IS...

"There is no reason to believe that Dad will not find another job – he **probably will find a job**."

"There is **no reason to believe** that we will lose everything because of this – but if we have to make some changes, **we will manage that**."

"There is **no reason to think** that my parents will start arguing about this – if that happens, **we can work it out. Things will get better**."

"This is not horrible – **it is unfortunate**."

MAKE A PLAN

MAKE A CONNECTION

IN THE END..Shim has helped herself.

Shim realizes that worrying about things **almost never helps.** In most cases, excessive worrying makes people **helpless and inactive.** Instead of worrying, Shim decides to **be concerned** about those rotten things that happen – and now she will be able to **make a plan, be helpful, be active.** She realizes, too, that it is healthier to **talk about** her concerns, and so she makes a good connection. She talks to her mom about all of this – and this makes her feel much safer, much happier. **Shim's SAT Plan helps her to change an unhealthy worry into a healthy concern.**

Practice and Share – Dad Losing His Job

My Picture	What has happened? **OR** What might happen?
STOP. RELAX. What other self-talk could help me **avoid over-reacting** to my father losing his job?	**THINK SENSIBLY. BE CALM. BE STRONG.** What other **positive self-talk** could help me think sensibly' about this?
MAKE A PLAN	**MAKE A CONNECTION**

IN THE END...What is Likely to Happen?
Be honest. Be realistic.

Lesson Thirty-four
Mom Getting Sick

Ⓐ INTRODUCTION

The Social Story in Lesson Thirty-four is about Vlad. Vlad's mom is sick and he is trying to get ready for exams. He is very, very worried.

Lesson Thirty-four shows that it is possible to minimize feelings of worry.

Ⓑ THE SCENARIO

1. Do a Guided/Shared Reading of Mom Getting Sick: When Emotions Take Over.
    Create a Discussion about Vlad's situation, his feelings, his reactions:
    • Vlad is stuck; he convinces himself that he can do nothing but worry. Do you agree?
    • Vlad decides to simply give up and accept failure (for the exam). What do you think about that?

2. Now do a Guided/Shared Reading using the S.A.T. Plan.
    Create a Discussion about Vlad's reaction this time:
    • Vlad is actively, strongly, bravely changing his attitude, his self-talk. How so?
    • Re-read Vlad's 4-part plan. Do you think he will be 100% successful with this?
    • Why is it a good-and-healthy move for Vlad to talk with Marietta about their mom?

3. Have students complete the practice page on this topic, and share their ideas with 2 or 3 others.

Ⓒ FOLLOW-UP

Suggested prompts for Journal Writing:
• Make a 5-point list entitled, "How to Worry Less."
• Can you make any connection to the story? Write about that.
• Write a short skit: Vlad talks to his sister, Marietta, about their mom's sickness.

When Emotions Take Over – Mom Getting Sick

Mom is sick and I don't know what will happen to us.

SCENARIO 34

Vlad's mother has become sick, and she has to stay in bed for several days. The whole family is upset about Mom's sickness – and this is especially true for Vlad. His exams are coming up, but Vlad can hardly concentrate on his work. Mom is sick and Vlad feels excessively worried.

NEGATIVE THINKING

Vlad is sitting at his desk, trying to study for next week's science test. But his brain is filled with **What will happen** questions about his mom's sickness:

"**What will happen** if mom doesn't get better?"

"**What will happen** to our family?"

"W**hat will happen** to me?"

Vlad cannot study. He can only think of his mom. All of his questions have no real answers and Vlad wonders if he will ever be able to pass his exam.

EMOTIONS TAKE OVER

Vlad's what will happen questions have taken over his brain – and each question seems to have no real answer. Since Vlad does not really know what will happen if mom does not get better, he imagines the worst. In his mind, he convinces himself that mom's sickness must be something that will result in some unbearable tragedy for his whole family.

These questions – with their uncertain answers – bring **excessive worry** to Vlad's mind.

THE UNDER–REACTION

There is nothing I can do about this. All I can do is worry, worry, worry.

THE OVER–REACTION

I can't concentrate on school. I am just going to fail my exam... I don't even care!

IN THE END...Vlad has not helped himself.

Vlad's emotional brain is clogged with **negative questions** – with uncertain answers. They are causing Vlad to get **bogged down in excessive worry**, and his two action plans are not helping things at all. If Vlad decides that he is **helpless,** he will be forever stuck in worry. If Vlad decides to **give up on school and fail,** he will have something else to worry about. Both of these action plans will doom Vlad to more worry – not less!

Doing nothing is a dangerous **UNDER-REACTION** – and the worry is growing.
Giving up and failing is a dangerous **OVER-REACTION** – and the worry is growing.

Using the S.A.T. Plan – Mom Getting Sick

Vlad is upset about his mom's sickness. But, he begins to question his own action plans. Are these plans really healthy? Will these plans make things better for him – or worse?

Vlad decides to put his thinking brain in control of all action plans. He decides to write up SAT Plan.

 STOP. RELAX.

Vlad begins to see that his **negative questions – with uncertain answers** are causing him to feel more worried than he needs to feel. He decides to stop all of these negative questions. When he begins to worry, he tells himself:

"Stop. Relax. Negative questions cause negative emotions. That is not helping."

Day by day, Vlad gets better at stopping the negative, uncertain self-talk. And, finally, he is able to substitute sensible, helpful, positive self-talk. More than anything, that is helping him to worry less.

 THINK SENSIBLY. BE CALM. BE STRONG.

Vlad re-examines his negative, uncertain self-talk and teaches himself helpful, positive self-talk.

THE TRUTH IS...

"I am going to **focus on Mom getting better**."

"I am going to **help my family deal** with this. This is a chance for us to **work together** and to help each other. This may make us **closer and stronger**."

"Whatever happens – **I will be okay. I will be strong and brave and helpful.** "

 MAKE A PLAN

MAKE A CONNECTION

IN THE END..Vlad has helped himself.

Vlad recognizes that those **negative questions** that he repeatedly asks himself are causing him to **worry excessively**. By actively stopping these questions and substituting **sensible, helpful, positive self-talk,** he **worries less**, and is able to make **better plans**. Vlad chooses to **be concerned** about his mom's sickness, but n**ot to worry excessively about something he cannot change**. Finally, Vlad connects with his sister; they have an honest talk about their mom's sickness. **Honest, open, straight-forward communication always helps. Vlad's SAT Plan helps him to stop fretting – and to start helping.**

Practice and Share – Mom Getting Sick

My Picture	What has happened? **OR** What might happen?
STOP. RELAX. What other self-talk could help me **avoid over-reacting** to my mom being sick?	**THINK SENSIBLY. BE CALM. BE STRONG.** What other **positive self-talk** could help me think sensibly' about this?
MAKE A PLAN	**MAKE A CONNECTION**

IN THE END...What is Likely to Happen?
Be honest. Be realistic.

Lesson Thirty-five
Losing an Object

Ⓐ INTRODUCTION

The Social Story in Lesson Thirty-five is about Celia. When Celia discovers that her favorite ring has gone missing, she becomes extremely angry and embarrassed.

Lesson Thirty-five shows that it is possible – and far more healthy – to supplant anger and embarrassment with a commitment to sensible thinking and positive action.

Ⓑ THE SCENARIO

1. Do a Guided/Shared Reading of Losing an Object: When Emotions Take Over.
   Create a Discussion about Celia's situation, her feelings, her reactions:
   • Celia convinces herself that she doesn't deserve nice things. What would you tell her?
   • Celia berates herself for being so stupid. What advice would you give her about that attitude?

2. Now do a Guided/Shared Reading using the S.A.T. Plan.
   Create a Discussion about Celia's reaction this time:
   • Re-read Celia's sensible thinking. Which self-statement do you think is most powerful?
   • Are there other positive self-statements that would be helpful for Celia?
   • Re-read Celia's plan. Do you think she can make a long-term commitment to that?

3. Have students complete the practice page on this topic, and share their ideas with 2 or 3 others.

Ⓒ FOLLOW-UP

Suggested prompts for Journal Writing:
• Write a mini-story about a character losing something important – and dealing with it very well.
• Can you make any connection to the story? Have you ever lost something important?
• How does one think positively about losing something important? Write about that.

When Emotions Take Over – Losing an Object

Oh NO! I lost that ring...I am so STUPID!

SCENARIO 35

Celia has lost her ring. This ring was very important to her; after all, it once belonged to her great grandmother. She has searched everywhere, but the ring is nowhere to be found. Celia feels **extremely embarrassed and extremely angry at herself.**

NEGATIVE THINKING

Whenever Celia thinks about the lost ring, she can feel her heart racing. And, her own self-talk is not very kind:

"I am so careless – **I don't deserve to have nice things**!"

"I lost great grandmother's ring – **I am so stupid.**"

"My mom and dad will **never forgive me** for this."

"I am **such a loser**!"

"What if Grandma finds out?"

EMOTIONS TAKE OVER

Celia knows that she has lost something very important to her – and also to her family. When she thinks about losing the ring, her self-talk is always very scolding and punishing. She convinces herself that she should not have valuable things; she brings herself down by telling herself how stupid and careless and reckless she is. All of these punishing self-statements cause her to feel **extreme embarrassment and extreme self-anger.**

THE UNDER-REACTION

I am not going to tell anyone that I lost that ring.

THE OVER-REACTION

If anyone bugs me about losing that ring, I will deny it. I will lie.

IN THE END...Celia has not helped herself.

Celia has **punished herself** over and over again with **scolding self-statements.** It is no wonder that she ends up feeling **extremely embarrassed and extremely angry** with herself. These **strong negative emotions** lead to a couple of plans. First, she thinks that **not telling anyone** will make the situation better; and second, she thinks that lying about the incident will make the situation better. Of course, they will not. Both of these reactions will lead to **more anger and embarrassment**, not less.

Not telling anyone is a less-than-brave **UNDER-REACTION.** The self-anger grows.
Lying about it is an irresponsible **OVER-REACTION.** The self-anger grows.

Using the S.A.T. Plan – Losing an Object

Hiding and denying are not the answers. Lying and blaming others are not the answers.

Celia thinks about her two plans. Is it really a good idea not to tell anyone about the lost ring? Is it really a good idea to lie about it to someone who might mention the lost ring?

Celia makes the decision to be brave and responsible. She writes up SAT Plan.

 STOP. RELAX.

Celia begins to understand that scolding herself over and over and over is not helping the situation. These scolding and punishing statements are only making her more embarrassed, more angry at herself. So, when these statements come into her mind, she tells herself:

"Stop. Relax. Scolding myself only makes me feel worse."

Slowly and steadily, Celia learns to stop scolding herself for losing the ring. She learns to talk to herself in a way that is more helpful, more positive.

 THINK SENSIBLY. BE CALM. BE STRONG.

Celia decides to use self-talk that is more helpful, more successful.
THE TRUTH IS...

"I may have been careless with the ring – **but I am a good person and I do deserve to have nice things**!"

"I lost great grandmother's ring – t**his does not mean I am so stupi**d. It means I lost the ring."

"My mom and dad will be **disappointed in me** for this, but **they will get over it. I will get over it**."

"Losing a ring does not make me – or anyone - a **loser**!"

MAKE A PLAN

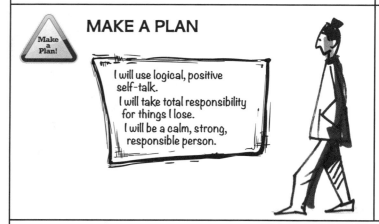

I will use logical, positive self-talk.
I will take total responsibility for things I lose.
I will be a calm, strong, responsible person.

MAKE A CONNECTION

Mom, I have something to tell you.

IN THE END..Celia has helped herself.
In the end, Celia has realized that **being mean to myself** for making a mistake is not a helpful thing. She comes to understand that **scolding myself over and over** is making her feel more embarrassed and angrier than ever – **and it is doing nothing to help the situation**. When Celia stops the negative, punishing self-talk, she is able to work out a **smart, successful SAT Plan**. And, when she bravely connects with her mom about this, she feels stronger and more confident. **Celia's SAT Plan helps her to accept what she cannot change – and to move on.**

Practice and Share – Losing an Object

My Picture	What has happened? **OR** What might happen?

STOP. RELAX. What other self-talk could help me **avoid over-reacting** to losing something valuable?	**THINK SENSIBLY. BE CALM. BE STRONG.** What other **positive self-talk** could help me think sensibly' about this?

MAKE A PLAN	**MAKE A CONNECTION**

IN THE END...What is Likely to Happen?
Be honest. Be realistic.

Lesson Thirty-six
Losing a Home

Ⓐ INTRODUCTION

The Social Story in Lesson Thirty-six is about Jarrod. Jarrod knows that money is tight for his family - and he can't stop thinking about it. He is filled with tremendous anxiety.

Lesson Thirty-six shows that it is possible to think calmly and rationally about difficult events – and thereby minimize stress and anxiety.

Ⓑ THE SCENARIO

1. Do a Guided/Shared Reading of Losing a Home: When Emotions Take Over.
    Create a Discussion about Jarrod's situation, his feelings, his reactions:
    • Re-read Jarrod's fears and nightmares. How do they make Jarrod feel?
    • Jarrod convinces himself that he will not be able to survive. Is that necessarily true?

2. Now do a Guided/Shared Reading using the S.A.T. Plan.
    Create a Discussion about Jarrod's reaction this time:
    • Re-read Jarrod's sensible self-talk. Which statement is the bravest?
    • Are there other positive self-statements that would be helpful for Jarrod?
    • Re-read Jarrod's 4-part plan. Could he add anything to that plan?

3. Have students complete the practice page on this topic, and share their ideas with 2 or 3 others.

Ⓒ FOLLOW-UP

Suggested prompts for Journal Writing:
• Create a Poster entitled, "If You Lose Everything" – with 5 helpful, healthy ways to cope with that.
• Put yourself in Jarrod's situation. What would you think and do? Write about that.
• How does one think positively about the possibility of losing his/her home?

When Emotions Take Over – Losing a Home

SCENARIO 36

Jarrod knows that money is tight in his home. He sometimes hears his mom talking about all of the bills they have to pay. For Jarrod it is an **everyday anxiety** - the **fear** and **nightmare** of losing their home and all of their money.

NEGATIVE THINKING

Jarrod works hard at school, and he has a part-time job to help his family make ends meet. Still, his mind is often visited by the fear whispers:

"You don't have much money. You might lose your home. You might lose the furniture. You might lose the car in the driveway. You might not be able to buy the clothes you want. You might not have enough food to eat. You will not be able to survive. You should be very upset."

EMOTIONS TAKE OVER

The fear whispers are never fair, never positive. They never have a balanced view of things. These whispers are always dark, negative and gloomy. For Jarrod, the worst time is at night, just before sleep – like nightmares.

These everyday **fears** and **nightmares** cause Jarrod to feel a great deal of anxiety.

THE UNDER–REACTION

I am worried – but I am not going to talk about these fears and night-mares. I am not going to tell anyone.

THE OVER-REACTION

Come here, rich kids. I will show you my fist!

IN THE END....Jarrod has not helped himself.

Jarrod's **fear whispers** are causing him **enormous anxiety**. But, his plan to **not talk about these fears and nightmares** will not help them to go away. His plan to **razz those kids** (who seem to have more money than he does) will only **create more problems**; this will lead to more conflicts with other kids – which usually mean **more anxiety**. Jarrod could use a plan that would help him to deal with the fear whispers and **lessen the anxiety** that he is feeling every day and every night.

Not talking to anyone is a smoldering **UNDER-REACTION**. The worry continues to weigh heavily. Razzing other kids, and fighting is a narrow-minded **OVER-REACTION**. The worry continues.

Using the S.A.T. Plan – Losing a Home

Hiding and denying are not the answers. Lying and blaming others are not the answers.

Jarrod reconsiders his two plans. He realizes that not talking to anyone is not going to lessen those fear whispers. And, taking it out on other kids is only going to add to his problems.

Jarrod decides to be smart and to take responsibility for his actions. He writes up a SAT Plan.

 ## STOP. RELAX.

Jarrod is beginning to see that his fears and nightmares are directly related to **what he is telling himself** over and over and over. He decides to put a stop to those dark, gloomy fear whispers. When he starts to feel anxious, he tells himself:

"Stop. Relax. I can manage whatever happens. My family will manage whatever happens."

Jarrod is learning to stop the fear whispers and to invite more reasonable, balanced, positive thoughts about the family's money difficulties.

 ## THINK SENSIBLY. BE CALM. BE STRONG.

Jarrod is realizing that his self whispers have a way of **horrible-izing** everything. Perhaps things are not so horrible after all.
THE TRUTH IS...

"There is no reason to believe that we will lose our home and all of our money – and thinking about that all the time **does not help**."

"If I have to, **I can learn to be happy with less money**. I can be **courageous** and **honest** about this."

MAKE A PLAN

1. I will BE HONEST about the money I have – or do not have.
2. I will STOP my dangerous, negative thinking.
3. I will ask some people on my street about a part-time job.

MAKE A CONNECTION

Jarrod has an honest talk with his mom.

IN THE END...Jarrod has helped himself.

Jarrod is seeing that, often, we all make up fears. And we need to understand that these fears are almost always deeply exaggerated thoughts. Fears make things much darker, and more negative than they really are. Jarrod is helping himself by refusing to believe these fear whispers and by reminding himself that things are not so horrible and that his family will manage like they always do. He talks to his mom about the money concerns in the family and that helps him to feel more relaxed.

Jarrod's SAT Plan is simple: he relaxes his mind and body and he thinks positive thoughts about the family. This helps him to stop the horrible-izing in his own mind – and the everyday anxiety becomes less and less and less.

Practice and Share – Losing a Home

My Picture	What has happened? **OR** What might happen?

![STOP Relax] **STOP. RELAX.** What other self-talk could help me **avoid over-reacting** to losing my home.	![Be Strong Be CALM] **THINK SENSIBLY. BE CALM. BE STRONG.** What other **positive self-talk** could help me think sensibly' about this?

![Make a Plan!] **MAKE A PLAN**	![Make a Connection] **MAKE A CONNECTION**

IN THE END...What is Likely to Happen?
Be honest. Be realistic.

Lesson Thirty-seven
Losing Parents

Ⓐ INTRODUCTION

The Social Story in Lesson Thirty-seven is about Annie. Annie is extremely worried that somehow, for some reason, her parents may die. And she cannot stop thinking about it!

Lesson Thirty-seven shows that it is possible to change "recurrent fears" into "legitimate concerns" – and thereby minimize worry and anxiety.

Ⓑ THE SCENARIO

1   Do a Guided/Shared Reading of Losing Parents: When Emotions Take Over.
    Create a Discussion about Annie's situation, her feelings, her reactions:
    • Is it normal and healthy to have concerns about the possible death of our parents?
    • Why do you think Annie has extreme fears and nightmares about her parents dying?

2. Now do a Guided/Shared Reading using the S.A.T. Plan.
    Create a Discussion about Annie's reaction this time:
    • Re-read Annie's sensible self-talk. In what way is it different from before?
    • Are there other positive self-statements that would be helpful for Annie?
    • Re-read Annie's plan. Is it realistic? Is it positive? How so?

3. Have students complete the practice page on this topic, and share their ideas with 2 or 3 others.

Ⓒ FOLLOW-UP

Suggested prompts for Journal Writing:
• A young child cannot stop worrying that his/her parents may die. Write him/her a helpful letter.
• Write 6 healthy, positive thoughts on "the possible death of one's parents."
• How does one think positively about the possibility of losing his/her parents?

When Emotions Take Over – Losing Parents

SCENARIO 37

Annie's parents are happy and healthy. Still, she has recurring fears and nightmares that something dreadful might happen to them. Her worst fear is that her parents may die. For Annie it is a constant worry – the **fear** and **nightmare** that her parents will suddenly die.

NEGATIVE THINKING

Annie does not know why, but it happens a lot: her mind is filled with gloomy thoughts of her parents dying.

"**What if my parents die**?"

"I will be **destroyed. I won't be able** to carry on."

"This will be the most **horrible, terrible, rotten thing**. "

"**I should worry about this! I must worry** about this!"

EMOTIONS TAKE OVER

Annie is noticing that her gloomy thoughts are more common at night, especially at bed time. During these times, she becomes focused on the ideas that her parents will die, and that she will be left to face the world alone, and that she will not be able to carry on.

These everyday **fears** and **nightmares** are causing Annie to be **constantly worried**.

THE UNDER–REACTION

I am going to keep my worries to myself. I won't tell anyone about my fears.

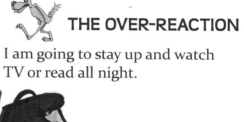

THE OVER-REACTION

I am going to stay up and watch TV or read all night.

IN THE END...Annie has not helped herself.

Annie's **gloomy thoughts** are causing her to constantly worry and to lose sleep. **Saying nothing is a dangerous thing** for Annie – it is very important to **talk to someone** about our worries and to **have a plan** to lessen these. **Staying up late** to watch television or read may help her for a while – but this is an **unhealthy plan** that will make her exhausted the next day. Annie needs a plan that will **lessen her worries** and help her to become a happier person.

Saying nothing is a short-sighted **UNDER-REACTION**. The fears and nightmares remain.
Staying up late" is an unhealthy **OVER-REACTION**. The fears and nightmares remain.

Using the S.A.T. Plan – Losing Parents

Annie knows that she is worrying too much. She knows, too, that hiding these worries from her parents is not helping. Plus, she is becoming overly tired from staying awake nights.

Annie wants a healthy, successful plan to help her lessen the constant worrying about her parents. She sits down and writes up a SAT Plan.

 STOP. RELAX.

Annie starts to examine her own negative self-talk. She is beginning to see that those overly gloomy, overly exaggerated thoughts are causing her to worry and lose sleep at night. When she starts to think about the possibility of her parents dying, she tells herself:

"Stop. Relax. These are silly, exaggerated ideas."

Annie is learning to stop her emotional brain from ruining her sleep. She is learning to relax her mind and body just before sleep and to focus on positive things.

 THINK SENSIBLY. BE CALM. BE STRONG.

Annie is beginning to see that her own self-talk is filled with exaggerations and untruths.
THE TRUTH IS...
"There is **no reason to believe** that my parents are going to die."
"Worrying about this **is not helpful**. It is **harmful.**"
"When I think about my parents, I am going to focus on **positive things**. I am going to remember **how much we care about each other**."
"At night I am going to **relax and take a deep breath**."

MAKE A PLAN

I am going to STOP my exaggerated worry-thoughts.
I will remind myself that I CAN manage whatever happens.
I will remind myself that my parents will probably be fine.

MAKE A CONNECTION

Ms. Tinsdale, I am always worrying about my parents' health. I am trying to stop worrying so much.

IN THE END..Annie has helped herself.

Annie's SAT Plan is helping her to manage her own thinking. It takes time and practice – but she can actively change her own gloomy self-talk into positive self-talk. Part of her plan is to get better at relaxing her mind and body just before sleep. She concentrates on positive images and relaxes her face, her arms, legs and body. And – she makes a connection with the school counselor. Ms. Tinsdale gives her some good advice about relaxing and thinking positively.

Annie is making sensible choices. She is realizing that nothing is certain in life – but it is much healthier to focus on positive things.

Practice and Share – Losing Parents

My Picture	What has happened? **OR** What might happen?
STOP. RELAX. What other self-talk could help me **avoid over-reacting** to an unrealistic fear?	**THINK SENSIBLY. BE CALM. BE STRONG.** What other **positive self-talk** could help me think sensibly' about this?
MAKE A PLAN	**MAKE A CONNECTION**

IN THE END...What is Likely to Happen?
Be honest. Be realistic.

Lesson Thirty-eight
Bullying

Ⓐ INTRODUCTION

The Social Story in Lesson Thirty-eight is about Jerry. Jerry occasionally experiences taunts and insensitive remarks from his classmates – a clear case of being bullied.

Lesson Thirty-eight shows that it is important to understand bullying for what it is – and that it is important to respond calmly and strongly to these behaviors.

Ⓑ THE SCENARIO

1. Do a Guided/Shared Reading of Bullying: When Emotions Take Over.
   Create a Discussion about Jerry's situation, his feelings, his reactions:
   • What is bullying?
   • Reinforce the definition: Bullying is when someone is being physically or verbally aggressive causing another person to feel upset, afraid, ashamed, embarrassed or worried. Bullying may include teasing, insulting, shoving, hitting, excluding, or spreading rumors.

2. Now do a Guided/Shared Reading using the S.A.T. Plan.
   Create a Discussion about Jerry's reaction this time:
   • What is likely to happen if Jerry does nothing about the bullying?
   • What is likely to happen if Jerry reacts calmly and strongly to the bullying behaviors of others?

3. Have students complete the practice page on this topic, and share their ideas with 2 or 3 others.

Ⓒ FOLLOW-UP

Suggested prompts for Journal Writing:
• You have a very tall friend who is constantly being teased about his height. Write him a helpful letter.
• Create a mini poster – that will be hung in the school hallway – about how to prevent bullying.
• Create a list of "10 Ways to Stop Bullying."

SCENARIO 38

Jerry hates going to school. Some of the boys in his class enjoy teasing him and shoving him into his locker. They think it is fun – but Jerry does not.

Jerry feels **constantly embarrassed** when he is teased and pushed around. He has a **constant fear** of being bullied.

NEGATIVE THINKING

Jerry has always accepted his classmates teasing and shoving, and his tendency is to have thoughts of helplessness' about it all.

"**I must be a real nerd. I guess I deserve the teasing and shoving.**"

"I am a loser. That's why I get teased all the time."

"There is **nothing** I can do about this. My classmates are strong and I am weak. **I am totally helpless.**"

EMOTIONS TAKE OVER

Jerry thinks about the teasing and shoving all the time. He thinks about it at night and has trouble getting to sleep.

Jerry's thoughts of helplessness are making him constantly **anxious** about going to school. More and more, he hates the prospect of leaving his house in the morning.

THE UNDER-REACTION

I am afraid to do' anything. I am afraid to say' anything. So I won't tell anyone about it.

THE OVER-REACTION

I will just CLOBBER those guys!

IN THE END...Jerry has not helped himself.

Bullying is when someone is being physically or verbally aggressive causing another person to feel upset, afraid, ashamed, embarrassed or worried. Bullying may include teasing, insulting, shoving, hitting, excluding, or spreading rumors.

Jerry's classmates are being physically aggressive and they are being verbally aggressive. Jerry needs to know that he is being bullied – and that everyone has the right not to be bullied! Jerry's **thoughts of helplessness'** are causing him ongoing anxiety about going to school. Saying nothing' is an unhealthy response – and it will only ensure that the bullying will continue. **Fighting back'** will only escalate the violence and he would likely be expelled from school; this will surely deepen his sadness.

Depending on what Jerry does, his problem becomes bigger or smaller. Saying and doing nothing' is a short-sighted **UNDER-REACTION**.

Fighting the bullies' is an unhealthy **OVER-REACTION**. Both responses won't stop the bullying

Using the S.A.T. Plan – Bully

I am afraid of being bullied, but I can't avoid going to school.

Jerry is trying to think sensibly about the extreme anxiety he has about getting bullied. He realizes that doing nothing and fighting back are doing nothing to solve the bullying problem. He needs a healthy, workable plan that will help him successfully deal with the bullying.

Jerry plugs in his thinking brain and creates a SAT Plan.

 ## STOP. RELAX.

Jerry knows that bullying is happening when someone is being physically or verbally aggressive causing another person to feel upset, afraid, ashamed, embarrassed or worried. Bullying may include teasing, insulting, shoving, hitting, excluding, or spreading rumors. Jerry knows he is being bullied. He tells himself:

"Stop. Relax. I am not helpless. I am not a loser. I have the right not to be bullied. I can think of a way to stop the bullying and ask for help."

Jerry reminds himself that it is possible to be calm and strong – rather than passive or violent.

 ## THINK SENSIBLY. BE CALM. BE STRONG.

Jerry is beginning to understand that his own feelings of helplessness' are preventing him from dealing with the ongoing bullying at school.

THE TRUTH IS...

"There is **no reason to believe** that I am a loser." "I have a right not to be bullied."

"Standing up to bullying makes it less likely to happen in the future; standing up to bullying calmly and strongly makes me feel better about myself."

"Asking for help dos not mean I am weak."

 ## MAKE A PLAN

1. I will stick up for myself in a calm, strong manner.
2. I will make eye contact and speak directly and honestly.
3. I will get help from a trusting adult.

MAKE A CONNECTION

I will go to see the guidance counselor at school. She can help me learn some other ways to stop the bullies.

GUIDANC

IN THE END...Jerry has helped himself.

Jerry's **SAT Plan** is helping him to stop all those **feelings of helplessness** about getting bullied. He is learning to become assertive with bullies – but not violent. Importantly, he is learning to stick up for himself' and that makes him proud.

Jerry is choosing to be smart about his reactions to bullying. He knows that there is no gain in feeling and acting helpless all the time. Jerry is learning that a strong and calm reaction is better than weak or violent' reaction. He also learns that asking for help is okay.

Practice and Share – Bully

My Picture	What has happened? **OR** What might happen?

STOP. RELAX. What other self-talk could help me **avoid over-reacting** to a bully?	**THINK SENSIBLY. BE CALM. BE STRONG.** What other **positive self-talk** could help me think sensibly' about this?

MAKE A PLAN	**MAKE A CONNECTION**

IN THE END...What is Likely to Happen?
Be honest. Be realistic.

Lesson Thirty-nine
Internet Safety

Ⓐ INTRODUCTION

The Social Story in Lesson Thirty-nine is about Brenda. Brenda spends a lot of time on her social media site – but she constantly worries that something bad will happen.

Lesson Thirty-nine shows that an attitude of "caution and safety" on social media sites is the best way to prevent those rotten things that could happen.

Ⓑ THE SCENARIO

1. Do a Guided/Shared Reading of Internet Safety: When Emotions Take Over.
   Create a Discussion about Brenda's situation, her feelings, her reactions:
   • What are social media sites? Why do people use these sites? What are some real risks?
   • Brenda is extremely fearful of using these sites. Does this help her in any way?

2. Now do a Guided/Shared Reading using the S.A.T. Plan.
   Create a Discussion about Brenda's reaction this time:
   • Is it appropriate for Brenda to be "concerned" about the risks on social media sites?
   • Brenda made an intentional, strong decision to stop worrying about what might happen on her own social media site. How did she do this?
   • Re-read Brenda's 4-part plan. How would such a plan defuse the great fears she is having?

3. Have students complete the practice page on this topic, and share their ideas with 2 or 3 others.

Ⓒ FOLLOW-UP

Suggested prompts for Journal Writing:
• Write a story about how the internet can be dangerous.
• List 8 thing to remember before sharing information on the internet.

I am so WORRIED that something BAD will happen!

SCENARIO 39

It is always on the news – people being bullied on internet social media sites; people being tricked into meeting someone. The risks associated with using social media sites are causing Brenda to be **constantly fearful.**

NEGATIVE THINKING

When Brenda thinks about the internet –and about all the bullying and dangers she hears her mind is filled with dark, negative thoughts:

"Bad things are **going to happen to me**."

"The internet is such a **terrible, rotten place**."

"People are going to write bad things about me and **my reputation will be destroyed**!"

EMOTIONS TAKE OVER

There are many good' things about the using internet – but Brenda does not think much about these. She convinces herself, over and over, that **the internet is a place of constant danger** – and that these bad things will surely happen to her.

Brenda's everyday thoughts about using the internet are causing her to be **constantly fearful**.

THE UNDER–REACTION

I will just avoid using the computer.

THE OVER-REACTION

I will lie about who I am when on the internet.

IN THE END...Brenda has not helped herself.

Brenda's mind is filled with **negative images**' about the internet. Her strategies' to cope with her constant fear are to avoid going on the internet' or to use another name when on social media sites.' These actions may make her own suffering a little more comfortable' – but she is **doing very little** to help her deal with these negative emotions over the longer term. Brenda could use a plan that would put her **thinking brain**' in control.

Avoiding the internet' is a shy, limp **UNDER-REACTION**. Brenda is losing out on the benefits. Posing as someone else" is a senseless **OVER-REACTION**. Brenda is just making matters worse .

Using the S.A.T. Plan – Internet Safety

Things will stay the same if I do NOTHING. Things will get better if I do SOMETHING.

Someone once told Brenda: "You keep on getting what you're getting, if you keep on doing what you're doing." Brenda decides to change what she is doing – and what she is thinking.

Brenda makes a change. She takes a pen and paper and writes up a SAT Plan.

 ## STOP. RELAX.

It becomes clear to Brenda that her own negative thoughts' about using the internet are causing her to live in fear. When those thoughts come into her mind, she tells herself:

"Stop. Relax. Be safe, be smart, be concerned – but don't worry all the time."

Over time, Brenda becomes an expert at stopping' the bad thoughts, and she becomes an expert in learning to relax.' Thinking wisely will help her to be safe when on the internet.

 ## THINK SENSIBLY. BE CALM. BE STRONG.

Brenda confronts her own negative images about using the internet:
THE TRUTH IS...

"I can be **concerned**' about internet safety – without being worried' about it.

"Instead of worrying, I can practice **cautious, safe behaviors** about using the internet."

"I am going to be smart about using the internet – but I am going to refuse to worry."

 ## MAKE A PLAN

I will NEVER
- send anyone my picture or personal information
- agree to meet someone I met online
- respond to any messages that make me feel uncomfortable
- send a rude or insulting message to anyone online

I will ALWAYS
- report any harassment or threatening messages to my parents
- set my browser to refuse "cookies"

 ## MAKE A CONNECTION

Brenda has a talk with her Mom. Sharing ideas reduces a lot of stress – that's for sure!

IN THE END...Brenda has helped herself.
Brenda's plan is to **think more wisely**' about the risks of using internet sites. Having an intelligent plan, she realizes, is better than constantly worrying. Brenda also makes an important connection about her concerns with internet safety – she talks to her mom and shares her **safety plan**.' Together they will stay safe and smart.

Brenda is learning to be safe, cautious and smart – instead of constantly worrying.

Practice and Share – Internet Safety

My Picture	What has happened? **OR** What might happen?

STOP. RELAX.

What other self-talk could help me **avoid over-reacting** to cyberbullying?

THINK SENSIBLY. BE CALM. BE STRONG.

What other **positive self-talk** could help me think sensibly' about this?

MAKE A PLAN

MAKE A CONNECTION

IN THE END...What is Likely to Happen?
Be honest. Be realistic.

Lesson Forty
Gossiping

Ⓐ INTRODUCTION

The Social Story in Lesson Forty is about Toshi. When Toshi finds out that some of the other kids in his class have been gossiping about him, he feels utterly humiliated.

Lesson Forty makes the point that gossip is a form of bullying – and that it is important to respond to gossiping rationally, calmly and assertively.

Ⓑ THE SCENARIO

1. Do a Guided/Shared Reading of Gossiping: When Emotions Take Over.
    Create a Discussion about Toshi's situation, his feelings, his reactions:
    • Toshi is feeling greatly humiliated (by the gossiping). What does that mean?
    • Do Toshi's "catastrophizing" thoughts help him in any way?

2. Now do a Guided/Shared Reading using the S.A.T. Plan.
    Create a Discussion about Toshi's reaction this time:
    • Toshi is reminding himself to be "realistic." What does that mean exactly?
    • Toshi made the decision to be "assertive" with the gossipers. What does that mean?
    • Re-read Toshi's 4-part plan. What if this plan does not work very well? What then?

3. Have students complete the practice page on this topic, and share their ideas with 2 or 3 others.

Ⓒ FOLLOW-UP

Suggested prompts for Journal Writing:
• What are some "assertive" ways to deal with gossiping?
• A good friend is a victim of some vicious gossip. Write a note to her/him – with some very helpful advice.
• What are your own thoughts and feelings about the subject of gossip? Write about these.

When Emotions Take Over – Gossiping

SCENARIO 40

Toshi finds out that some of the kids in his class have been saying mean things about him behind his back. "Why are the kids gossiping about me? Don't they like me?" These questions are causing him feel **greatly humiliated.**

NEGATIVE THINKING

Toshi's mind is swimming with unkind thoughts about the bullying:

"They are talking about me behind my back... They **must hate me**! They must think I am a **total jerk**!"

"This is the worst thing that has ever happened to me. I can't stand this!"

EMOTIONS TAKE OVER

Toshi has gotten into an unhealthy habit' – he constantly thinks about the gossiping and how it has made him feel.

Toshi's negative thoughts about the kids' gossip are causing him to feel humiliated – and angry at the kids.

THE UNDER–REACTION

I will not tell anyone about this. It's so embarrassing.

THE OVER–REACTION

I will teach those jerks a lesson! I will make up gossip about them.

IN THE END...Toshi has not helped himself.

Being gossiped about is a rotten thing for sure. But Toshi's unproven, negative thoughts are making the rotten thing much more rotten. These thoughts are increasing his feelings of embarrassment and humiliation.

Never mentioning his fears to anyone' is a wrong **UNDER-REACTION**. The problem just gets bigger. Making up gossip about the other kids' is an **OVER-REACTION**. The problem just gets bigger.

Using the S.A.T. Plan – Gossiping

I will be FAIR.
I will be BRAVE.

Toshi realizes that if he does not act with FAIRNESS and COURAGE, nothing will change – and he will continue to be afraid that people are gossiping about him.

Toshi makes the decision to write up a SAT Plan – filled with COURAGE and FAIRNESS.

STOP. RELAX.

Toshi reminds himself that being gossiped about is wrong and unfair – and there is no need to feel humiliated about that. When the negative, hurtful self-thoughts come, he tells himself:

"Stop. Relax. Be realistic."

Toshi knows that the first step of a SAT Plan is to stop all negative, hurtful thinking. He learns to do this by **telling himself** to stop thinking this way. The more he practices this skill, the better he gets.

THINK SENSIBLY. BE CALM. BE STRONG.

Toshi thinks about the negative thoughts that come into his mind.

THE TRUTH IS...

"Being gossiped about does not mean that everyone hates me...**It does not mean that I am a total jerk**. My true friends don't believe it."

"Being gossiped about is a rotten thing, but **it is only disappointing; I can manage this; I can be strong and assertive**. If others want to believe the gossip I can't stop them."

MAKE A PLAN

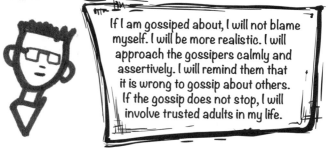

If I am gossiped about, I will not blame myself. I will be more realistic. I will approach the gossipers calmly and assertively. I will remind them that it is wrong to gossip about others. If the gossip does not stop, I will involve trusted adults in my life.

MAKE A CONNECTION

Toshi makes an appointment with the school guidance counselor. He wants to get some ideas about what else he can do to respond to the gossiping.

IN THE END..Toshi has helped himself.

Part of Toshio's SAT plan involves (a) not blaming himself (b) thinking more realistically' about what being gossiped about really proves, and (c) responding to gossipers calmly and assertively.

Toshi is learning to stay positive and to kick out those unproven, exaggerated thoughts that can sometimes cause feelings of humiliation. He is learning to act with calmness and assertiveness when treated wrongly and unfairly. He realizes that sometimes you need to get help from others.

Practice and Share – Gossiping

My Picture	What has happened? **OR** What might happen?
STOP. RELAX. What other self-talk could help me **avoid over-reacting** to hearing gossip?	**THINK SENSIBLY. BE CALM. BE STRONG.** What other **positive self-talk** could help me think sensibly' about this?
MAKE A PLAN	**MAKE A CONNECTION**

IN THE END...What is Likely to Happen?
Be honest. Be realistic.

OUR LEARNING SPACE CREED

This is our **LEARNING SPACE**. In this space we are all equal and we all have rights. I can expect that for myself. I will honor that for others.

I HAVE A RIGHT TO BE SAFE AND COMFORTABLE.

• In this space, no one may cause me injury or discomfort. This includes the right to have my property left alone and undamaged.

• I will honor every other person's right to be safe and comfortable.

I HAVE A RIGHT TO LEARN.

• In this space, I have the right to think and to concentrate. No one has the right to disrupt me or make it difficult for me to learn.

• I will honor every other person's right to learn.

I HAVE A RIGHT TO BE HEARD.

• In this space, I have the right to share my ideas. No one has the right to interrupt me when it is my turn to speak.

• I will honor every other person's right to be heard.

I HAVE A RIGHT TO BE RESPECTED.

• In this space, I have dignity. No one has the right disrespect me with their words or actions.

• I will honor every other person's right to be respected.

COACHING MYSELF – WITH FAR BETTER THOUGHTS

Good coaches are important. They give us the right advice; they help us to build confidence in ourselves; they support us – even when we mess up. Good coaches are always on our side.

In truth, we can be our own good coaches. We can give ourselves the right advice, we can help ourselves to be more confident, and we can forever support ourselves – even when we mess up.

I am always coaching myself through my own self-talk. When my self-talk is negative, unproven and self-defeating, I am going to experience a lot of stress and self-doubt. But, when my self-talk is wise and positive and supportive, I will deal with life's rotten events much better. If I am my own best coach, I will have less worry, less guilt, less anger, and less stress. And that is far better!

Here are 10 far better thoughts – that are wise, positive and self-supporting. Get to know them; practice them; get good at them. Be your own best coach.

1. **I am unique. I am good.**

    I am living in a very material world, where advertisements on television and magazines are constantly telling all of us to buy more and more things, and to constantly compare ourselves to others. In our society, there is often a lot of pressure to have more stuff in order to fit in, to be popular. This is a dangerous life-attitude. When I constantly compare myself to others, I will always feel unworthy. After all, there will always be people who have talents I do not have, or who have more money, or who look better, or who are more popular.

I will coach myself to have a healthy, positive life-attitude. I will remember that we are not what we own. Each of us has strengths and weaknesses. I will not compare myself to others. I am who I am. I am a unique person in the world. I am not perfect – but I am good. This is a far better life-attitude.

Life isn't fair. Get over it. Move on.

Rotten things sometimes happen. People sometimes do rotten things. Life is sometimes less than fair. That's just the way it is. When I demand that the world should always be fair, or when I tell myself over and over that people should be fair all the time, I will always feel helpless and frustrated. This can be very stressful.

It is far better to coach myself that rotten things sometimes happen, that life is not always fair, that people are not always fair. I can accept that, get over it, and move on.

Be calm. Be strong.

I know that when a rotten thing happens, I always have a choice. I can choose to yell and scream and threaten and fight – but such over-reactions almost always make the rotten thing more rotten. I can withdraw from people and sulk and do nothing – but such under-reactions never make the rotten thing less rotten. Or, I can choose to act calmly and strongly.

When something rotten happens, it is far better to coach myself to be calm and strong. If I can stick up for myself and take action in a way that shows coolness and strength, things always turn out better.

Don't hate. Always forgive.

I can certainly choose to hate people when they are rotten to me. I can try to get back at them and try to make them feel bad – just like they made me feel bad. But hate only piles up, and getting back at others never really teaches them a lesson at all – it only makes them hate me more and it makes them want to get back at me all the more. Worse than that, is the fact that hating others is very heavy, very draining, very stressful.

Refusing to hate is a brave choice. Forgiveness is a brave choice. When I coach myself to forgive, I am breaking the never-ending cycle of hate. It is far better, far less stressful, to walk the halls with a feeling of peace and forgiveness than to walk the halls with hatred and feelings of revenge.

Be patient. This will pass.

When a rotten thing happens, it seems to fill me up like water fills a sponge. I often think that this will be rotten forever, or I will be sad about this for a long, long time. These thoughts can be very stressful, and they might very well cause me to panic.

When I feel completely swallowed up by some rotten happening, it is helpful to coach myself to be patient, to remind myself that this rotten thing will pass. I need to remember that time heals all wounds – it really does. Don't panic, be patient – this is far better.

Find a quite space. Breathe deeply.

It is sometimes very difficult to be myself. There are times when my living space is very busy, very hectic, very stressful – and during these times it becomes very difficult to think calmly and to make my own decisions.

When I feel that my world is becoming too busy and stressful, I will coach myself to look for a quiet space, where I can calm down, think sensibly, and breathe deeply. I know that it is not always possible for me to leave an uncomfortable place, but whenever I can go to a place that is peaceful and quiet, I am able to relax my whole body, breathe deeply, be myself – and that is far better.

7. **Don't jump to conclusions. Don't assume the worst.**

   When I am not included in a conversation, I may be tempted to think the worst – that people don't really like me. If I am not hired for the job I wanted, I might think that no one will ever hire me. If I fail a math test, I might think that I am stupid. Such conclusions are unproven, gloomy, and self-hurting. When I jump to conclusions, and assume the worst, I am setting myself up for sadness.

   Whenever I feel rejected, I will coach myself to stay confident, stay positive. I will ask myself: What does this really mean? What does this really prove? Jumping to conclusions is dangerous and self-defeating. It is far better to think sensibly and assume the best.

8. **Lighten up. It's not the end of the world.**

   I may have a tendency to – at least sometimes – awfulize or horriblize or terriblize some rotten thing that has happened to me. If I tell myself that a rotten event is truly awful, horrible, terrible, then it becomes that – and I am then likely to feel tremendous sadness or anger or frustration. My own horriblizing self-talk has the power to make a rotten happening a lot more rotten.

   In the face of a rotten event, I will coach myself to stop awfulizing – and, instead, to lighten up. It helps to remind myself that most things are not awful-horrible-terrible – they are only unfortunate or annoying, or a little troubling. It helps, also, to remind myself that most rotten things are not the end of the world. I can teach myself to lighten up or to see some humor in it - and that is far better.

9. **Work to change those things that can be changed. Don't sweat those things that cannot be changed.**

   It is possible to get bogged down about things that seem rotten. I might become very frustrated about the amount of noise in my neighborhood, or about how tall or short I happen to be, or about my parents' divorce – things that I really cannot change. When I constantly fret about these unchangeable things, my life can be very stressful.

   It makes sense to try to change those things that I can change, especially when they will lead to my overall happiness. But, clearly, there are things that I really cannot hope to change. I can coach myself not worry about those things that I don't have much chance of changing. I will actively refuse to worry about those unchangeable things – and that is far better.

10. **Do not fear failure. Take a chance. Go for it!**

    I may want to pass on opportunities that would actually help me to grow or to add to my happiness – especially when those opportunities risk failure. I might think that if I don't try out for the team, I won't risk failing to make the team; if I don't perform the guitar solo in front of an audience, I don't risk them laughing at me. It is very tempting to stay in my comfort zone, to not take chances, to not risk failing.

    When something is important to me, I will coach myself to move out of my comfort zone. I will take a risk – especially when the risk involves my personal growth and happiness. I will not be afraid of failure. I will congratulate myself for having the courage to take a chance – and that is far better.

References ///

Benard, B. (1991). *Fostering Resilience in Kids: Protective Factors in the Family, School and Community*. Portland, OR: Northwest Regional Educational Laboratory.

Csikszentmihalyi, M., & Larsen, R. (1984). *Being Adolescent*. New York: Basic Books.

Curwin, R. L., & Mendler, A.N. (Rev. ed. 1999). *Discipline with Dignity*. New York: Association for Supervision and Curriculum Development.

Daniels, H. (Ed.) (1996). *An Introduction to Vygotsky*. London: Routledge.

Dreikurs, R., Grunwald, B.B. & Pepper, F. (1971). *Maintaining Sanity in the Classroom*. New York: Harper and Row.

Ellis, A. (1973). *Humanistic Psychotherapy: The Rational-Emotive Approach*. New York: McGraw-Hill.

Garfinkel, B., Hoberman, H., Parsons, J., and Walker, J. Adolescent Stress, Depression and Suicide: Minnesota study. Unpublished raw data, 1986.

Gibbs, Jeanne. (2001). Tribes: A New Way of Learning and Being Together. Windsor: Center Course Systems.

Goleman, D. (1995). *Emotional Intelligence*. New York: Bantam Books.

Hall, Melissa. *What? Me worry? - children's worries* - adapted from *Child Development*, June 1996 http://findarticles.com/p/articles/mi_m0816/is_n8_v16/ai_18763100. Accessed: August 20, 2006

Kerr, R. (1987), *Positively! Learning to Manage Negative Emotions*. Portland, ME: J. Weston Walch, Publisher.

Kerr, R. (1999). *Self Discipline: Using portfolios to help students develop self-awareness, manage emotions and build relationships*. Markham: Pembroke Publishers.

Kerr, R. (1997). *The Superlative 21st Century Classroom*. Portland, ME: J. Weston Walch, Publisher.

Kerr, R. (1995). *Stop and Think: Empowering Students to Manage Behavior*. Portland, ME: J. Weston Walch, Publisher.

Levine, M. (2001). Jarvis Clutch – *Social Spy: Enabling children and adolescents to improve their social cognition. Guidelines for Use.* Cambridge, MA: Educators Publishing Service.

Smetana, J.G. (2011). *Adolescents' social reasoning and relationships with parents: Conflicts and coordinations within and across domains.* In E. Amsel & J. Smetana (Eds.), *Adolescent vulnerabilities and opportunities: Constructivist and developmental perspectives,* (pp. 139-158). New York: Cambridge University Press.

Steinberg, L. (2008). *Adolescence*. New York: McGraw-Hill.

Walker, Joyce (2005). *Teens in distress: adolescent stress and depression.* Website: University of Minnesota: Center for 4-H Youth Development. http://www.extension.umn.edu/distribution/youthdevelopment/DA3083.html

Anxiety, fears, and phobias. Website: Kids Heath for parents. http://www.kidshealth.org/parent/emotions/feelings/anxiety.html

CASA 2003 teen survey: high stress levels, frequent boredom, too much spending money: triple threat that hikes risk of teen substance abuse (2003). Website: The National Center on Addiction and Substance Abuse at Columbia University. http://www.casacolumbia.org/absolutenm/templates/PressReleases.aspx?articleid=348&zoneid=46

Children's worries take new shape. The Washington Post Company. http://www.coping.org/911/healing/kids/kidart.html

Deborah Smith. Everyday fears trump worries about terrorism. American Psychological Association website: http://www.apa.org/monitor/may03/everyday.html

Dealing with a crisis. Website: Parenting and child health. http://www.cyh.com/HealthTopics/HealthTopicDetails.aspx?p=114&np=141&id=1560

Dr. Andrew McDowell in "Our young are lying awake' with worry." http://www.samaritans.org.uk/support/247/press210506a.shtm

Fears and phobias – older children and teenagers. Website: Parenting and child health. http://www.cyh.com/HealthTopics/HealthTopicDetails.aspx?p=114&np=141&id=2295

Keep kids healthy.com. A paediatrician's guide to your children's health and safety. http://www.keepkidshealthy.com/parenting_tips/fears.html

Leah Davies. Helping children cope with worries. http://www.kellybear.com/TeacherArticles/TeacherTip6.html

"Maximizing learning: A conversation with Renate Nummela Caine." Educational Leadership. Vol. 54, No6, March, 1997.

Press Release: OHSU Research reveals likely connection between early-life stress and mental health problems during the teenage years (November 16, 2005). Website: Oregon Health and Science University. http://www.ohsu.edu/ohsuedu/newspub/releases/111605stress.cfm

Science News: Increase incidence of migraine headaches (1995). Website: Science Daily. http://www.sciencedaily.com/releases/1999/10/991025075957.htm

Teenagers and Stress. Gateway Cooperative Extension Service, University of Illinois. http://web.aces.uiuc.edu/vista/pdf_pubs/GW11.pdf

Wake-up call over teen stress (2005). Website: University of Ulster. http://news.ulster.ac.uk/releases/2005/1523.html

War and children. Website: Parenting and child heath. http://www.cyh.com/HealthTopics/HealthTopicDetails.aspx?p=114&np=141&id=1909